ESSAYS OF A STRING TEACHER

Books by Clifford A. Cook

Essays of a String Teacher
Suzuki Education in Action
String Teaching and Some Related Topics

Essays of a String Teacher
Come, Let Us Rosin Together

Clifford A. Cook

An Exposition-University Book
Exposition Press   New York

Dedicated to

MIA STELLA

Contents

Preface

An old violin contained the following inscription (in Latin): *Arbor viva, tacui, mortura, cano* ("When I was part of a living tree, I was silent; now dead, I sing").

When the writer was in the midst of the hurly-burly of a busy teaching career, there was little time for writing or thought. Retirement brings greater opportunity for thinking back and writing. This book is then, in a sense, autobiographical. It covers different periods and fluctuating interests. Its many phases occurred at various times, not all at once.

In the past, string study and scholarly writing often have had two "requirements" in common. First, they must be dull (preferably monumentally dull). Second, they must be painful (preferably excruciating). The long trek across a desert of dry études or through a dismal swamp of endless footnotes was sustained only by a faint hope of eventually reaching some sort of Promised Land! Hopefully, both of these requirements are being relaxed a bit now.

Any list or bibliography is obsolete by the time it appears in print, because new things are constantly appearing. But reflection on "What's new?" brings interesting conclusions. How many times might a program item read "Last performance," as well as "First performance"? What is the survival ratio of new things? One out of one hundred? How much experience is necessary to understand the deep meaning of "ephemeral"? What wisdom Shakespeare packed into his lines beginning "All the world's a stage—"!

This book is my third on the strings, and my final one. As I told a reporter: "It's like baseball; three strikes and out." At any rate, here it is.

9

ESSAYS OF A STRING TEACHER

Chapter I

Thoughts on Private Teaching

I

Recently a plumber spent five minutes making a slight repair in my bathroom. No new part was involved. The bill for this service was twelve dollars. At this rate of compensation, a half-hour job would cost seventy-two dollars!

Most music teachers have at least as much professional preparation as the average plumber has. Investment in tools of the trade, such as a fine violin, a grand piano, and an extensive library of music, should balance the cost of the plumber's required equipment. But what music teacher can charge twelve dollars for five minutes of his professional service? Surely the conscientious music teacher's lessons at three, five, or seven dollars are a great bargain today! (And aren't music students as important as what flows through the bathroom pipes the plumber repairs?)

II

What is a *good lesson*? From the viewpoint of the child a good lesson is one in which the assignment is played in such a way that the teacher finds little to criticize. This *is* one type of good lesson.

But may not a lesson also be "good" when it contains considerable criticism as well as praise? Helpful advice and instruction concern improvement of faults and weaknesses, as well as pointing out virtues and building confidence. It is in a delicate balance of praise and shock treatment, correctly adjusted for each student, that the music teacher shows himself to be an astute psychologist.

What was learned in the lesson? (It's not just a matter of how well the student played.) The child and his parents have the right to ask this question about each lesson: *Did we get our money's worth?*

III

High-pressure and low-pressure teaching—both have proved successful; each has failed with certain students not adapted to such instruction. Even the best pitchers don't win all their ball games or the best hitters get a home run every time at bat! Likewise, the music teacher can't expect to "win them all." He should teach in the way that is natural for him, that expresses his own true personality.

IV

Short lessons with some master teachers:

Ottokar Sevcik's students say his great gift was that he taught them how to practice and to think for themselves.

Leopold Auer: "One great point I lay stress on in teaching is never to kill the individuality of my various pupils. Another great principle in my teaching is to demand as much as possible of the pupil. Then he will give you something!"

Leon Sametini: "The mistake made by so many teachers is that they unfortunately try to cover too much territory. We would all be much better off if the teacher would not teach beyond that which he has thoroughly studied and mastered himself."

Georges Enesco never seemed concerned with time in his teaching. He showed a sense of eternity, difficult for a busy teacher to acquire.

Pablo Casals has the capacity for staying at a thing endlessly until it is "right." According to one of his artist-students, Casals' lessons were like "peeling an onion." As the student finished playing a selection, Casals complimented him, "but . . . ." The selection was repeated; again a compliment was followed by another "but . . . ." This process went on until the student was exhausted.

Ivan Galamian has maintained a teaching schedule of such intensity and success as to merit being called a fanatic on violin teaching. His enthusiasm and persistence in solving each problem for his students are well known. He says: "The teacher must be even in temperament, not subject to moods. I remember when I was studying. Sometimes I would practice very hard and go for a lesson which I thought would be a good one. The teacher was in a bad mood. He would tell me I had a terrible lesson. Perhaps another time I would not practice at all. The teacher was feeling fine. He would tell me I had a good lesson. Such a situation should not be. A student soon wonders why he should practice at all! The pupils are more sensitive than we think they are."

Albert Schweitzer has written that "there is a modesty of the soul, as well as of the body." Let the teacher beware of "playing God" with his trusting students, or their disillusionment may follow.

V

The artist is concerned with his own problems, the teacher with other people's problems. When an artist first turns to teaching, considerable groping is likely to result along two lines: (1) a tendency to rely excessively on his own playing *for* students, setting up a model and letting it go at that; (2) emphasis on *one thing* as the answer to all problems—finger movement, wrist motion, or whatever the panacea of the moment may be!

A recent panacea advocates *concentration on the base joints of the fingers of the left hand,* even for bowing problems. One more popular musical panacea: The idea that music must be "always going somewhere"—constantly getting louder or softer—more intense or more relaxed—is great for avoiding monotony or dullness in performance. But this idea can become a fetish in teaching, unfortunate and inappropriate at times, when overdone.

VI

Older, experienced teachers are likely to develop "hardening of the methods," to build rigid "machines" in their teaching through which *all* their students must pass. "He who dares to teach must never cease to learn." To maintain a fresh outlook in teaching, to study each pupil as a unique individual, to avoid applying *idées fixes* to all one's students—these problems loom before the teacher with growing intensity as the years roll by.

VII

Beyond a certain point, every teacher has no more to contribute to an advanced student's artistic career. One of the most difficult decisions to make (and carry out) is determining the correct answer to this question: When and where should one send a gifted student for further study with another teacher? It is one of the most soul-searching questions a conscientious teacher has to face.

VIII

Fortunately, teaching is not altogether solving problems. Many unforeseen moments of pleasure appear during lessons. As I was starting a lesson with a youngster who was embarking on her exploration of positions on the violin I asked, "Are you beginning to feel at home in the third position?" Quick as a flash came her answer: "Well, it's a new apartment!" My chuckle told an old story—once again *teacher* had learned something.

Chapter II

Notes on String Class Teaching

A letter to *The Strad* magazine in 1896 says ". . . There is also the system of class tuition, which, in my opinion, ought to be put a stop to; I think it is a perfect shame that such a system should be allowed to exist. . . ."

Recently, after a college class had observed instrumental music instruction in a city school system, where a number of beginning string classes were heard, one serious student wrote, "I now have no desire to teach music in public schools." Apparently, some of the problems of string class teaching are not yet solved any better than they were about seventy years ago in the "old country."

Brief quotes from three friends, all concertmasters of professional symphonies: No. 1, hearing a school class, "Not an F♯ in the bunch!" No. 2, in an address: "Now we come to the dirty words—'music education.'" No. 3, in an interview, referred to the "cripples produced by music education." These are a few of the more printable quotes; the majority in my large collection are *un*printable.

A brief word on the other side of the picture. In this time of mushrooming "Centers for the Performing Arts," when it seems that every music school and music student in our country is specializing in the "highest standards of excellence *in performance*," I have only one comment. If we are to take this whole thing seriously, at least 95 per cent of the people currently "in performance" have no business there!

Now, back to class teaching. Classes of string instruments in England are listed at least as early as 1840. Karl W. Gehrkens wrote that about 1905 in the village of Maidstone, County of Kent, England, an experiment was made to see whether violin playing could be taught to classes just as sightsinging and other subjects are. The movement spread, and eventually tens of thousands of children all over England learned to play the violin through class instruction.

There seems to be general agreement that Albert G. Mitchell was the first violin class teacher in the United States. In 1911 he introduced in Boston schools the class plan he had observed in England. Karl W. Gehrkens offered class work in violin in the Oberlin public schools circa 1915, "after Charles Farnsworth's enthusiastic account of thousands of English children playing violins in Crystal Palace, London, with many additional thousands studying the violin in classes all over England." Don Morrison came to Oberlin and began teaching string classes in 1916.

Class teaching of the strings has been practiced for well over one hundred years, and the violin class method has set the example for the teaching of many other instruments. Present economic conditions seem to indicate that class teaching will continue and expand. Public schools simply cannot afford the luxury of paying a teacher full salary for the private teaching of thirty one-hour pupils per week.

Both private and class teaching may be poor, mediocre, or good—there is no difference in respect to quality potential. Each system has its place, aims, and demands; the two systems should be complementary, not antagonistic. Of course, management and instruction of a class place greater demands and burdens on a teacher than do individual, private lessons. Not all teachers can cope with merely controlling groups of students, let alone trying to teach them anything.

Every orchestra conductor in the world does a form of class teaching. What is objected to in many cases (assuming the teacher *is* capable of handling groups successfully) is teaching by someone who doesn't really know his subject, who has had only a little smattering of instruction in it, teaching by people who are expected to teach almost everything in music—an impossibly broad assignment.

Much string class "material" (it can't be called "music") has been slapped together and turned out in a hurry, and with little thought or care. Its frequent poor quality (sheer junk at times), condescending style, mistakes by the bushel give little cause for pride in the "composers" or publishers, and imply that this field is not worthy of a good job—"close enough for jazz," as the hacks put it.

Gertrude Collins in England and Elizabeth Green in America have written serious books on string class teaching, as have the two Ralphs, Matesky and Rush. Paul Zahtilla's *Suzuki in the String Class* (Summy-Birchard) is just coming out as this is written.

The primary aim of string classes is to develop string orchestras which will provide the foundation for later full orchestras. To achieve this aim, viola, cello, and bass must be taught. The remarkable Suzuki school in Japan has produced large numbers of violinists, but it has not as yet developed many players of the other string instruments needed for orchestras. Indeed, production of orchestral fodder has never been Suzuki's primary purpose.

One of the most common faults observed in the teaching of string classes consists of giving extended semiprivate lessons while the rest of the students are unoccupied (or are *very* soon occupied with extracurricular activities). Keeping *all* the students meaningfully occupied practically *all* the time should be the aim. Effective class routines keep playing in progress while individual corrections are made.

Fundamental playing postures of the students, intonation, and tone are the basic problems in string classes. Playing postures may be silently and individually corrected by the teacher while the class plays.

But for intonation and tonal checking frequent individual playing *is* necessary. Here is an example of a technique for hearing individuals without turning the rest of the class free for mischief: One student plays arco, the others pizzicato. A few more —solo arco, tutti "act" fingering or bowing; solos by phrases, skipping around class as teacher points; duets and larger ensembles with one player on a part; solo playing for class criticism. The class teacher needs many such techniques at his instant command.

The objection is frequently raised that individual differences are often so great in a string class that private lessons or individual teaching seem the only way out. There are ways of adding difficulty to unison parts for more advanced players, when splitting a class into sections is not possible. On scales and arpeggios, one-, two-, and three-octave ranges may be used simultaneously. An open string part may be played with various harmonics. A too-easy part may be transposed an octave, a first-position part may be played in other positions. A treble-clef violin part may be read by the viola player, whose alto-clef part is too easy for him. Bowing variations may be played by more advanced students.

Beginning ensemble music breaks up the unison approach; string orchestra music is available for all levels from the very easy, as found in the excellent Polychordia String Library. The Vaughan Williams *Concerto Grosso* is a fine example of simultaneous parts ranging from difficult down to open strings. (It is no accident that the music just mentioned is of English origin.) Combining string classes in projects such as the Corelli-Purcell-Vivaldi units later described in Chapter XIV provides worthwhile musical experiences coupled with *musical* learning (appreciation in the best sense of the word).

Keeping up all phases of string playing in classes is important. It is easy to neglect bowing, for example, unless plans are carefully made. Written comments on individual playing checks provide a record of the common problems which persist. The best check on how well fundamental habits are established, comes when concentration is on one element in playing—for example, check bowing when a student's attention is centered on intonation, and vice versa.

From written criticisms of playing checks of one hundred students in various string classes, here are the ten most common defects (in diminishing order of frequency) in the use of 1) the bow, and 2) the left hand and arm, with a few suggested remedies:

Bowing (often more faulty than left hand)

1. Bow skids or slides on string (not grooved).
   A. Two pencils or teacher's fingers make a slot for the bow while student draws it. Or teacher holds his bow to make a "guard-rail to keep the student's bow on the highway."
   B. With correct hold of bow (which is maintained in playing position on various strings by teacher), the student smoothly glides his fingers from one end of the bow to the other to get the feel of a straight line in bowing. (Or *Bowrite* gadget may be used for this purpose.)
   C. Bow-screw is aimed at a target on the wall in such a way that a correct stroke is made.
2. Bow does not *move* enough (stiff, grabby grip inhibits movement).
   A. The key here is loosening all the joints involved in the bow hold and stroke, then developing a feel of flow and easy movement in drawing the bow.
3. Bow circles (crooked, not at right angle to strings—often goes with No. 1 above).
   A. Be sure the bow is not too long for the student's arm (mark the "tip" with chalk, if it is), and be sure the relationship of instrument and bow are correct. Then apply the same remedies as for No. 1.
4. Wrong contact point of bow on strings (too far toward fingerboard or bridge—habitual *sul tasto* or *ponticello*.)
   A. Usually what is needed is an adjustment in where the instrument is held, so the bow contact point will come naturally at the right spot.
5. Tilt (wrong way—toward bridge; or right way, but excessive, so wood touches string).
   A. If bow-hold is reasonable, excess in bending or caving of the wrist must be corrected. Focus eye-attention on relation of stick to hair and strings.
6. Neighboring strings sideswiped by bow (Leopold Stokowski listed this as a principal defect in symphony auditions).

    A. Check cut of bridge. If correct, use eye-control to help develop feel for planes of strings.

    B. Play much in a dark room, or with eyes closed.

    C. Watch out for excessive motion during change of bow or string.

7. Tone not clear (weak—bow not *in* string).

    A. Work to get more weight into the bow, more feel of "hanging" in the arm.

    B. Practice "pinching" the bow while it rests on a string, to force the wood down to the hair. Practice staccato and martelé attacks.

8. Caved and stiff thumb and little finger. Especially common in members of the double-jointed fraternity.

    A. If the normal slightly curved position of thumb and fingers cannot be sustained due to weak double-joints, try maintaining an extremely bent thumb and pinky until their joints are strengthened somewhat. Then try the normal bend in the joints. Extremely caved joints will *never* become flexible.

9. Overpressure (wood forced on hair or string).

    A. Work to relax joints; develop soft part of dynamic range. Concentrate on lengthwise movement of bow, not pressure into strings.

10. Loss of tone toward point of bow (weight in string not adjusted to keep sound even).

    A. Develop more strength in upper half of bow. Start at tip, lean into the string before moving bow. When tone is solid in upper half, practice whole bows with necessary adjustment of weight to keep tone even.

    In good playing, the bowing results from the expression called for by the music. In poor performance, the expression comes from the bowing.

There are many more faults, such as tremble in middle of bow-stroke, teacup hold with *pinky en l'air,* bow not rationed correctly, etc., but the above ten are most common. Eye-control is needed in correcting certain of the faults; a comfortable hold of the bow and a correct feel while drawing it are needed in all ten cases.

Left Hand and Arm

1. Not sure of fingerings and spacing ("fishing fingers").
    A. Finger patterns and spacing intervals *must* be learned, as well as pitch intervals. Otherwise, pitch is purely a matter of trial and error. There is both "absolute and relative" pitch for the fingers, too! "Recite" fingerings and finger-spacing to be used.
2. "Humoresque"—lack of coordination between finger and bow changes.
    A. Stop bow, change finger or string or both, draw bow. Gradually reduce length of bow-stop until it is not noticeable.
3. Hand crawls, loses its place, causing modulation—"hand-modulation."
    A. Do not release old finger until new finger's tone is sounding, to avoid shifting hand from note to note.
4. Hand not placed and shaped so fingers can reach.
    A. Watch that elbow and arm adjust with hand to place groups of fingers over the spots they must stop on the strings. The string palindrome—spots=stops.
5. Thumb-hand relation wrong.
    A. Place the thumb so it will help the fingers accomplish their task, not hinder them. This must be an individual adjustment.
6. Faulty hold of instrument as a whole.
    A. Hold of instrument should be comfortable, yet secure, in order to leave the left hand and arm free to function efficiently. Another individual matter, requiring correct choice of chin rest and shoulder pad, if needed.
7. Overshifting (faulty grouping of notes).
    A. Flash-card reading practice to grasp groups of notes.
    B. Top note of passage is usually fingered with top finger.
    C. In sight-reading, don't shift more than you have to. The

first time around, if first position will do it, fine.

8. Grabbing neck of instrument, "strangulation" (tight hand—excessive tension in general).

   A. Same as for No. 6. Even on violin, the base of the first finger may have to be kept clear away from the neck of the instrument, so grabbing is impossible.

9. "Saucer"—palm of hand against neck of the instrument.

   A. Practice in upper position where the hand is against the instrument and correctly shaped (as when playing the half-string harmonic with fourth or third finger). Then bring hand, in same shape, down to first position. Violin must not be supported by palm of hand.

   B. Imagine the scroll is a magnet, pulling left wrist back towards it.

10. Fingers not kept down when they should be ("piano fingers").

   A. Practice keeping all fingers down after dropping them in order on one string; then reverse, lifting fingers in order, to make same series of pitches in reverse. Then put all fingers down at once on one string; lift them in order, making descending pitches. (But block-fingering or grabbing must not be overdone or it leads to tension and stiffness. And cantilena playing calls for the fewest possible fingers on string at a time!)

There are many more defects such as caving fingers, sagging instruments, vibratos which shake the instrument and bow into a weird dance, etc. But the above ten faults proved most common.

String class teachers can learn much about techniques for class management from observing skilled academic class teachers who know how to keep *all* students on their toes while individuals recite or are heard and checked.

Chapter III

More on Suzuki

(This chapter continues beyond my book, *Suzuki Education in Action*, Exposition Press, Inc., 1970. Appendix B of the present book presents a Short Selected Bibliography on Suzuki.)

The annual October tours by Japanese Suzuki students have continued. In addition to their usual coast-to-coast appearances in the United States, the 1970 group of children performed in Berlin, London, and Lisbon for the first time, with "Same impact as first time in States," according to Dr. Honda. The 1971 tour included Sweden, Ireland, other English cities as well as London—Scotland and Canada, plus the United States. In 1972, five sold-out concerts in England preceded the tour of the United States and Canada. The tour programs now include piano and cello solos as regular features. Interest in the Suzuki movement is today truly worldwide.

The Strad magazine (London) for June 1971 contained a review of my Suzuki book. As my reply was not published, the review and reply are now presented:

Review. Reports of a wonderful system of group teaching of the violin in Japan have been filtering through for years, and an account of the method by one who has been directly associated with it promised to be of prime interest. Unfortunately it appears to be not so much a book on the subject as a collection of articles written for advertising purposes, both the style and content being typical of the press handout. The author went to Japan for talks with Shinichi Suzuki about his method of "Talent Education" (which apparently can be applied to other subjects than violin playing) and took back Suzuki graduates to teach at Oberlin College in the United States.

This is not an easy book to read; the greater part of it consists of rather nauseating gush about the marvellous results of the

25

system. To find out what the system is, we plough through 100
pages of this, only to discover that the author does not intend to
tell us. We gather that children are made familiar with music
by listening continually to recordings, and that they learn to play
by ear. If a child cannot answer a question while playing a piece
without missing a note he is told "more work! You don't know it
yet!" which seems to indicate that the intelligence plays no part
in this method. A hint on exercises for control of the bow is significant, but scarcely original. Professor Cook himself appears to
believe that no American (and therefore presumably no European) will ever fully understand Suzuki Talent Education, but
if it is really true that it is possible to get a group of 1200 children
playing well with not a poor left-hand position or bow-arm visible,
there must be some physical method by which it is achieved,
and it is disappointing to find oneself still in the dark after reading this book. A.D.

Reply.

Oberlin, Ohio
July 12, 1971

Please publish

Dear Strad:

I wish to thank you for the thoughtful and penetrating review of my book, *Suzuki Education in Action,* by A.D. (at least
it was not B.C.) on page 65 of your issue for June, 1971. This
review was an unexpected pleasure, as I had not included your
magazine in my list to receive review copies. Please permit me to
explain why.

In 1962 I visited the Strad office in London and talked to
the editor. When I told him I was going to Japan to visit Shinichi
Suzuki, he replied, "We have seen pictures of masses of Japanese
children playing violins—they remind us of Hitler's youth meetings!" Later, after my return from Japan, I wrote an article ex-
plaining the Suzuki movement and sent it to your magazine. It
was returned with a note saying you couldn't use it.

I therefore concluded that *The Strad* had little interest in
the string movement in the Orient, but would continue to spark
interest in string playing and listening through its practical books
such as *La Casa Nuziale* (1962). (Fortunately, the English string
playing I heard did not inspire me to write any of my "rather
nauseating gush about the marvellous results of the system.")

I was, then, much surprised to read in the June *Strad* of reviewer A.D.'s anticipation of my book and great disappointment after reading it to find himself still in the dark about the physical method involved in the Suzuki way of holding the left hand and the bow arm. It's really *not* an Oriental mystery or a secret, A.D., old chap! Every one of the touring Japanese children used this physical method when they played in London last Fall, and questions about it were answered following the concert.

Anyway, thanks again to A.D., *The Strad,* and the unknown donor of my book. With best wishes for your continued and valued leadership in the flourishing World of Strings, I am,

Sincerely,
Clifford A. Cook (or C.A.C.)

As a final note on this subject, here are reviews from London newspapers after concerts by the touring children in October, 1971:

Daily Telegraph, London, Oct. 5, 1971

Concerts

The secret of playing it by ear

The extraordinary success achieved by the Japanese teacher Suzuki, with his method of training for young musicians, particularly young string players, was demonstrated in convincing fashion at the Queen Elizabeth Hall last night.

Ten of his pupils—youngest aged nine, and eldest fourteen—brought tremendous confidence to the whole business of playing, from the first application of bow to string, to tiny details of phrasing and tone.

Always their ear for sound seemed unusually alert, no doubt because this method is rooted in early ear-training by direct imitation, rather than by reading music from the written page.

All the children in fact played from memory throughout the programme and it was noticeable that, for instance, in unison playing, they were able to produce remarkable uniformity of sound.

Thus, the five violinists in a Rondo by Mozart, or the eight who played the Largo from Vivaldi's Concerto Grosso in D minor, approached the pieces as one player.

But any fears that perhaps this method might ultimately lead only to imitation and conformity were allayed by the musicality of the young girl playing the first movement of Beethoven's Violin Concerto. N.K.

The Sunday Times, October 10, 1971

Music for everyone
Felix Aprahamian

The week in which for the very first time an Emperor of Japan visits London has had its appropriate musical reflection at South Bank: Japanese conductor, composition, traditional instrumentalists and, most auspicious of all, last Monday's Queen Elizabeth Hall concert by Japanese children ranging from nine to fourteen years of age.

The Talent Education Method of teaching the violin initiated by Dr. Shinichi Suzuki thirty years ago has produced something unique. The perfectly disciplined string-playing of these young people rightly held the large audience spellbound. It was a strangely moving musical experience. No allowances had to be made for their execution of a well-known Vivaldi siciliano and presto: both were impeccable. There were remarkable individual violin performances of the first movement of Beethoven's Concerto and of Bach's solo Chaconne. An eleven-year-old cellist threw off Popper's Gavotte with style and assurance.

Is the Suzuki Method a kind of broiler-house for string-players? The present supply of musically mature Japanese violinists now available to European orchestras as well as the tone, intonation, technique and expressiveness of our young visitors disposes of such a criticism. Next year, the Rural Music Schools Association, with some generous Leverhulme and Gulgenkian aid, begins a five-year programme of investigation into the Suzuki Method and its possible application here. The results could be far-reaching.

To review briefly the fundamentals of Suzuki Education, a few remarks were made from these notes of mine at the Ohio String Teachers Association "Suzuki Day," May 16, 1971:

Basic Principles of Suzuki Talent Education

Now to attempt to penetrate some of the Oriental mysteries—a bit like Edwin Newman's attempt to analyze the ingredients of tempura in a Japanese kitchen: "Unidentified frying objects."

Traditional way of teaching music in the Orient is "viva voce"—by *sound,* somewhat like teaching a blind person. Blind school of koto players *(sharp ears)* and blind massage experts and acupuncturists *(sharp sense of touch)*—combine these two and you have *Suzuki Talent Education.*

PRINCIPLES

I. *Based on the way we learn to speak our "mother tongue."* Do we give tests to babies to decide which can learn to speak English? (Then say: "This one can, this one can't—*send to Italy!*") In musical training a very small circle may be drawn, to *exclude* many. Or a large circle may be drawn, to *include* all who wish to play. *But we can't draw a tiny circle and then ask "Where are the audiences and support?"*

Who ever learned to speak by his eyes? Which birds learned to sing by reading? The birds are full of song at this time of year, but there are very few music stands in the trees!

II. *Very early start in music.* Two tiny babies—Jonelle Keranen, Negaunee, and Chizu Kataoka, St. Louis—are both well along in Talent Education. Talent Education of babies reminds me of the tiny desert saguaro, which can grow and develop properly only when protected by a paloverde or other tree. *Good environment essential*—parental interest, encouragement, love as well as protection. (Note changes due to environment— the same H_2O may be water, ice, or steam, depending on its environment, as Dr. Honda writes.) An early start is especially needed on violin, probably the most *unnatural* of all instruments. The violin is ideal for early start in that it comes in many sizes, and the unnatural hold and playing techniques are much easier for the very young to acquire.

Many prodigies who were pushed unmercifully by their parents, teachers, or managers later had "breakdowns." Some were able to rework their way out. Others *never* recovered. Much more research is needed on the subject of wise, very-early education of children!

III. *Ear-training first*—development of sensitivity. The child who defined "arco" as what you hear when you play in an empty, bare room was at least *listening*. Neglect of the ear—not hearing what you're after—is a very common fault in string playing. Where there is no regular listening to good models, no solfège, *nothing*, how can we expect a child to know what he's after in pitch? Spontaneous combustion?

Memory training is important, also. *Haiku:* seventeen syllables, "wordless poetry," invites the listener to participate, instead of leaving him dumb with admiration while the poet shows off. *Roji*—garden path leading to tearoom; "Idea of the Roji":

> *A cluster of summer trees*
> *A bit of the sea*
> *A pale evening moon.*

Another *haiku,* by a child:

> *Wind-bells tinkling ring*
> *All the while dear grandpapa*
> *His siesta takes.*

Haiku are used for memory training, and later for creative expression. (Eiko Suzuki knew by memory one hundred *haiku* when she was four.)

IV. *Reactions sharpened constantly*—by fun and interest. Gymnastics, games, tests, always suited to child's age and level, just as the violin used fits child's size. Note on the difficulty of adult thinking of little child's world—Menuhin to a young boy at a lesson: "Too monolithic!" (He also said "The printed page gets in the way of the *music!*")

Talent Education works for Total Concentration. (California has many faults, but there's nothing like an earthquake to develop Total Concentration. As the Hollywood studio violinist said to the orchestra during the abrupt silence produced by an earthquake: "At least, we'll die with our mutes on.") An earthquake is one kind of tremolo that commands *undivided attention!*

V. *Instruction by ear goes to Vivaldi Concerto and beyond, then reading is gradually introduced.* No rush about reading. Go at child's pace, no pressure. Patience—the impressive, giant saguaros grew *very* slowly. Mother Nature has patience—why can't we have more of it? Encouragement. Love and respect.

VI. *Thorough mastery of each step,* one thing at a time. 100 times 0=0; 1 times 1=*1*. Repetition—"The Mother of Knowledge." *Meaningful repetition* takes on new meaning with Suzuki (making hundreds of diplomas, or *sumi-e* paintings, by hand before dawn,—setting one hundred and fifty soundposts a day, when in Junior High School—repeating a point in teaching until understood and *right*.) Hear and practice same piece over and over, "not English, French, Italian, German, and Japanese on successive days."

Add, don't finish. Improve what is already known, build *ability.* Note the "Journey of *Perpetual Motion*." Develop to capacity—realize potential. William James: "Compared with what we ought to be, we are only half awake. We are making use of only a small part of our physical and mental resources. Stating the thing broadly, the human individual thus lives far within his limits. He possesses powers of various sorts which he habitually fails to use."

Development of *character,* good person. Shinichi Suzuki puts "the heart before the course," as does Pablo Casals.

VII. *Music becomes part of oneself, easy, natural, like speaking, a normal part of life.* There are no "dropouts" from speaking English here today! (But some hypercritical people remind me of Oscar Wilde's reaction to Niagara Falls: *"Nifels would be more impressive if the water ran the other way!"*)

The Summer 1971 issue of *Talent Education News* contained this little article:

Some Common Errors In Teaching Suzuki In America
("We learn from failures, not successes."—Marvin Rabin)

Clifford Cook, Oberlin, Ohio

There is almost a 100% lack of Saino-Kyoiku tone and finesse. We need to practice tonalization much more.

Use of only the "fun and games" approach. This is easily overdone. We need further understanding of how much hard work has been done by the Japanese children whose playing we admire.

Misunderstanding of the meaning of "Talent Education." It means education to bring out latent talent, not the education of children selected by "talent tests." There is some tendency to make Suzuki study an elite proposition (snobbish and very expensive), open only to the wealthy. This is completely contrary to the Suzuki philosophy.

Indifferent use of records or tapes, or use of poor mechanical equipment (Audio-Visual Hindrances).

Attempts to teach Suzuki without parental (or "in loco parentis") involvement—doomed to failure with little children.

Too much stress on competition.

Overemphasis on the physical part of playing. The key to Suzuki is not primarily physical.

Very early reading from music while playing. Vibrato from the beginning of study. Such "improvements" on the system are not really improvements at all! Skipping about among the pieces and books of the Suzuki method often results in poor preparation for playing advanced pieces. ("Hit and run" teaching. Note Tyrone Guthrie's advice to young actors: "Take a breath and do one thing at a time.")

Many children are heard struggling with pieces they are not prepared for. Some teachers obviously do not realize how carefully Suzuki builds, step by step.

Failure to understand how long young children can stay at a lesson or piece without getting tired or bored.

Insufficient attention given to the piano part—this is very important! A good introduction and a musical, sensitive accompaniment make much difference in string performance.

Impatience and lack of discipline (teachers, parents, children.) A nagging, negative approach rather than a positive one.

Poor teaching (usually to large groups of children) produces some playing with no standards at all. Large class instruction as the basic teaching procedure is simply not Suzuki! A rather low general level of teaching shows little real comprehension of the Suzuki principles. This field should not be a haven for unsuccessful teachers, or for poor quality graduate students! Nothing is overlooked as much as the obvious. Many teachers either don't know Suzuki or don't really believe him. They don't understand that he means practice exactly what he preaches!

Great enthusiasm for Suzuki's philosophy of producing fine people rather than professional musicians is shown by some teachers because it gets them "off the hook"—*is used as an alibi for poor results!*

Two Japanese teachers, thoroughly experienced in teaching Suzuki in the States, express their thoughts on the matter:

Teacher No. 1: American parents leave it to the children to decide what they do and how much; the parents don't discipline and guide the children enough.

Teacher No. 2: In Japan, Suzuki's philosophy and basic ideas are much studied, thought about, and discussed; here, the important thing seems to be to get children to play violin while very young.

A photograph on the bulletin board outside a teacher's studio showed an adorable baby lying in a violin case. The caption was "Suzuki Method." There is, however, much more to Talent Education than the cute pictures.

The First American Suzuki Institute was held the last week of July 1971 at Wisconsin State University, Stevens Point. The writer's keynote speech included these remarks:

In a recent television travelogue about the Basque shepherds' country, it was pointed out that all their houses have two or more doors. Why? *They don't want to put all their Basques in one exit.* Those of us here today have obviously decided to put our "string eggs" in the basket of "Suzuki Talent Education." However, we must take good care of our eggs in *any* basket, lest, as when ducks fly upside down, they *quack up!*

This American Suzuki Institute is a unique event, the first time so many Americans with great diversity of background have attempted to create an "American melting pot" of Talent Education experience on our own, without the physical presence of our little Japanese friend with the magnetic personality and the pixie-like qualities which appeal so much to children and adults alike. He has sent us a message. Here is the voice of Shinichi Suzuki [Suzuki's tape played].

As we have tried since 1958, in our various ways, to translate the Japanese language and mores, and the experience, philosophy, and psychology of Mr. Suzuki and his coworkers into our own, we have encountered many questions and problems. The first came with the translation of the Japanese name for the movement, *Saino-Kyoiku.* The translation most commonly used, "Talent Education," has misled many Americans into assuming that this movement involves first, the identification and selection of children with inborn talent; second, the intensive musical education of these selected, tested children. This concept would be accurate for the Russian system, but as we well know, it is completely erroneous when applied to Mr. Suzuki's ideas about what talent really is.

Not much experience is required to make us realize that in comparing the East and the West we get into a very broad and complicated subject. (I don't mean simply that an American in Hong Kong may Wing the Wong number!) Our record of reading the Vietnamese mind is hardly impressive, to say the least. The many fine violinists now coming from *Korea* (not just Japan) provide food for our thought. And I suspect that we're going to be learning a lot more about China in the near future. (*How true!*) Recently newspapers carried a picture of Chinese children with this caption written by a Western visitor: "*Sing Along—* These kindergarten children perform a song-dance routine. *Even at this early age, their movements seem to reflect the discipline required of soldiers or professional dancers.*" Apparently, the Chinese are doing more than playing table tennis!

Our communication problem has not been limited to differences between the East and West. A magazine editor changed the title of an early article I wrote on Talent Education, so that it came out as "Genius by the Gross," implying that geniuses would pour out from this movement like water from a spigot. The changed title led to an embarrassing question from the Dean of my school, after several years of instruction: "How many geniuses have you turned out so far?"

The most recent embarrassment to come my way is a scathing review of my Suzuki book in *The Strad* magazine. The reviewer laments his conclusion that "the author does not intend to tell us what the Suzuki system is," and his final anguished remark reads: "If it is really true that it is possible to get a group of 1200 children playing well with not a poor left-hand position or bow-arm visible, *there must be some physical method by which it is achieved,* and it is disappointing to find oneself still in the dark after reading this book." My friends, for heaven's sake, while you're here this week, *be sure you learn the physical method used to hold the violin and bow—then you'll have the secret key to the entire Suzuki system!*

Other misunderstandings about the aims and claims of what we are trying to do have been too numerous to mention here. A prime purpose for this week together should be clarification of these aims and claims. The vitality of Mr. Suzuki's ideas and

their results is shown by both the extreme devotion and the viru-
lent criticism he has inspired. (*Aside*—Thomas Edison once made
a study and said the more education you had the less likely you
were to become an inventor. If Mr. Suzuki had received only a
little more education, he would have *known* that what he did
couldn't be done!) No one can fully assess the impact of the
Suzuki movement in the United States in these thirteen brief
years. One can only surmise how great and far-reaching it has
been.

May I address a few words to the parents of children here
today? We hear much about "Gifted Children." A few reflections
about children who are *really* gifted: These are the fortunate
children whose parents have made them gifts beyond reckoning
of value, such as

> Love and security.
> Interest, time, and patience.
> Enduring discipline, persistence in work habits.
> Appreciation and encouragement, self-confidence.
> The best environment possible, showing by con-
> tinuous investment of time, money, and interest
> what the parents consider most worthwhile in the
> good life desired for their children. (Money alone
> is not enough, as in the case of the doctor's wife
> who regrets her investment in a $3,000 Liebe-
> straum for her son.)

For the teachers present, a few thoughts now on the subject
of "The Musical Deep Freeze (or Embalmed Performance) in
the Machine Age of Music": The freezer provides many musical
meals—records or tapes are "frozen sound" and movies or photos
are "frozen sight." After hearing the horrible sound on some films
(bunch of kazoos), and the impractical pitch and tempi of some
records (recalling the impossible English in the first Japanese
Suzuki books), one realizes that in addition to valuable audio-
visual *aids,* there may be also some audio-visual *hindrances!*

The importance in the Suzuki method of good musical ma-
chinery and paraphernalia (phonographs, projectors, records,
tapes, etc.) calls our attention to some of the common problems
encountered in using this equipment. The doctored performances
heard on records and tapes present a standard almost unattain-
able in live performance and put a premium on note-perfect
rendition. As Mr. Suzuki says, a record cannot change, grow, or
improve. The splatter-sound of the violin's open strings on records
does little to win converts to our instrument. It has led to the

fanatical rule of some teachers: *Never* use an open string if it can be avoided. There is no need to list the many mechanical problems involved in successful operation in the Machine Age. Automation is with us in music, as in industry. Certainly, in my own experience, provision and maintenance of satisfactory mechanical equipment have rated right along with the human factors in providing the good environment sought for our young beginning violinists.

Most important of the people at Stevens Point this week are the children. They are the reason for our being here, and our success will be measured primarily by what we can do for *them*.

There is no person in this room who cannot learn something from every other person in the room. During the week, let us all share, help, learn and teach to the best of our ability. We'll then have a wonderfully rich and broadening experience. I close with the title of a stirring March many of us have played: *On, Wisconsin!*

Finally, let us pay tribute to the person whose vision and persistent hard work have brought us together for this unique experience: Professor Margery V. Aber.

Many video tapes were made of the teaching and concerts at the Institute. During the final months of 1971, the writer compiled the following document, which may partially satisfy the Strad reviewer who wanted more intimate physical details about the Suzuki method:

Composite Report From The American Suzuki Institute

The first American Suzuki Institute was held at Wisconsin State University, Stevens Point, Wisconsin, July 25-30, 1971. About three hundred and fifty children, parents, students, and teachers from the United States and Canada were registered, and several hundred other parents and spouses also attended. The faculty of twenty members comprised American and Japanese Suzuki specialists from ten states.

A written report of observations made during the week was required of all the participants who received credit for their week's work. This article consists of a compilation of extracts from the reports of many teachers and college students, observing all the faculty members at work with children in individual and group lessons, and hearing panels, concerts, etc., throughout the week.

Of course, the "silent majority" of participants were not concerned with college credit—a healthy sign! One notes that in the amount of material written the order of importance is 1. general and philosophical teaching procedures, 2. the bow, 3. the left side.

Perhaps this summary will provide a "bird's-eye view" of the Institute for those who were not able to attend, and give a broader perspective than any individual attending could achieve personally. If so, it will be worth the considerable time and effort it took.

A Few Quotes

"It was a very full and stimulating week, and I wonder if we can ever again manage to have so many of the top echelon together. Through the years that I have been teaching and interested in Talent Education these were its forefathers, its pioneers, the strong pillars of its U.S. development."

"The faculty was a most fortunate combination of young Japanese-trained teachers and fine experienced American teachers who through their devotion and dedication to fine string teaching had been converted and were now ardent, enthusiastic Suzuki teachers."

"All teachers were teaching Suzuki philosophy with the violin, but each brought his own imagination to the presentation. Each teacher has varied ways of saying the same thing many times. The relationship of teacher to student is 'Nurtured by Love.' "

"I have heard that the Suzuki ideology is a giant machine turning out hundreds of smaller violinistic machines, each almost exactly like the other and with little claim to individuality of its own. The week proved this wrong."

"The Institute convinced me that I am not presently qualified to teach this method, but it is definitely worth the effort to *become* qualified."

"I learned that many of the approaches and procedures that I was using that I thought were Suzuki designated, were *not necessarily so.*"

"My child benefited greatly (in spite of the broken arm). We plan to cage David up six weeks preceding the Institute to make sure he has *two* arms next time!"

"There was no printed music at a music institute!"

"Obvious respect was shown for the dignity of the children attending."

Teacher: "There's nothing wrong—just try it this way."

Child in cello class: "The better we get, the more people expect of us."

"The emphasis on fine playing was good for public school teachers, beset by problems of schedule and organization."

"More emphasis was needed on public school teaching."

"Why switch to Suzuki? One would have to be both blind and stupid to see and hear the Suzuki children and not realize that what they were doing was right. Just listen to the results of the Suzuki children from Japan."

"Hearing familiar pieces played in recital by Eiko Suzuki Kataoka made each one seem refreshingly new and beautiful."

"The Fiddlin' Square Dance added new spice to old pieces."

"Too much 'hurry up—and wait!' "

Private lesson: "Teacher's voice is so soft it's hard to hear, but there is a feeling of warmth and communication."

"An inspiration for teaching of *any* kind. It affected my piano teaching immediately. There are many parallels in life and Talent Education. *Much food for thought—I haven't stopped thinking, and won't.*"

"The final concert, with teachers and students from nearly all the U.S. playing so beautifully together, made a wonderful way to end such an inspiring week—one we will always remember."

Philosophy

(One teacher writes that he now has two phases in his interpretation of the Suzuki approach: Musical and philosophical.)

"I discovered that Suzuki has a whole philosophy of education which affects all education, not just violin playing."

Mr. Suzuki writes: "My prayer is that all children may become fine human beings, happy people of superior ability. I am convinced that all children are born with this potential."

"The attitude of expecting excellence from the children while at the same time being relaxed and having fun was most exciting. *Maintain high standards in a pleasant atmosphere.*"

Humor in a lesson is a necessary ingredient.

Suzuki is not necessarily training musicians, but boys and girls to be noble human beings.

Talent Education is not a method. Consider it a total human development. "We teach the *Suzuki approach*—not a group approach."

Quality is the keyword—of tone, musicality, and practice.

The future of the human race depends on the understanding of how infant human beings emerge from early shapelessness to the phenomenal powers of the formative years.

Time to start?—the earlier, the better. *Grow* into playing. The child will then always feel comfortable on the instrument, it will always stay with him. Young children grow faster and sponge up learning quicker.

What we "grow into" feels more natural—so, the violin is learned by *osmosis*, like the English language. Violin is going on around us all the time.

The important thing is not how many years you've studied, but how much you've practiced.

Success is not running through a bunch of pieces, but preparing the child for the future.

Self-direction is the goal, but *structured learning* must precede. *Be satisfied with going slow.* Parents and teachers are too goal-oriented. The child should enjoy the *process.* (Teacher, too!)

Do the Suzuki philosophy and the present trend in education conflict? No, much self-discipline is needed in today's modular system of education. Suzuki trains for this.

Meaningful repetition is very important—practice a troublesome passage 5,000 times! How long will the children stand repetition? As long as the teacher!

"It is important to be able to play musically before learning to read."

Why give manufactured exercises (printed études), when there is so much great music?

Pressure diminishes our chance to grow.

Shotgun Education is *have to*. Talent Education is *want to*.

Children absorb the feelings of adults. *Smile.* Timbre of voice is important. Speak slowly, do not shout. Do not sound impatient. When the body is tight, the voice is tight.

Children learn by paying attention, visually, aurally, and by memory retention. Forced memorization speeds technical improvement.

No amount of listening and watching can replace actually doing it yourself. Learning is not just thinking, but experiencing and acting. Beauty, sensitivity and excellence are valued as desirable personal qualities as well as desirable playing qualities. Suzuki does not aspire to produce people who play the violin beautifully, but rather beautiful people who also happen to play the violin.

"It is very apparent that the success or failure of the Suzuki approach has as its key the degree of parental involvement." "Parent participation or no lessons" is not possible in many public school situations, however.

Students must learn to *stop*—stop to think and prepare, stop to correct.

"Our society not only encourages, but *congratulates* mediocrity! We can do better than that."

More creativity is possible in a regimented system, through invention of tunes, etc. Mr. Suzuki: "The child *catches* all the time in today's education. He should *pitch* some, too!"

Do the Suzuki children play like machines? Speech is also learned by imitation. After the basic patterns are learned, children are free to be expressive with the tools they have developed. Freedom is achieved through control.

Comparison of Japanese and American Children

Japanese	*American*
1. Much homework	1. Varies
2. Few activities	2. Many activities
3. Great respect for authority and age	3. Less (little) respect for authority and age
4. Adjust easily to mixed age groups [not always—C.C.]	4. *Very* peer conscious—prefer own age group
5. Receive much help from parents	5. Receive less help—parents usually *too busy!*
6. Rapid progress, commensurate with daily practice	6. Progress is slower—less practice

Some Questions with a few Answers

Teacher to student: "How do you want it? Whom do you have to please? Me? Your mother? No—*yourself!*"

Parent's question: "Will my child be spoiled by all the attention she gets now as being a special person, and then some day wake up and find she's a nobody?" Reply: "You can't give your child too much self-esteem. She is unique and a special person. Nobody is a nobody. The goal is to make every person a fine and noble human being, not constantly seeking to be No. 1, with the most prestige, power and money. Let's rather have competition to be the finest human being."

Observer's questions: Does the Suzuki method require an exceptional teacher? Is performance the ultimate goal? Does today's philosophy of education conflict irreconcilably with Suzuki's?

What is the advantage of group playing? You must *keep going.*

Parent: How can I handle a child who doesn't want to practice? Suggestions: 1. Establish a pattern, a definite practice time each day as discipline. 2. Use an early hour, before school. 3. Use psychology: "Come, play for me as I iron—it relaxes me."

4. Parents' *attitude* is important. 5. Several smaller sessions, until child tires. Gradually increase. 6. Tapes of practice sessions may be brought to teacher for suggestions. (Affluent society?)

What happens to Suzuki players after high school? We'll have to wait and see, we're not that far along yet in the States.

Is "Momism" developed with very close relationship of mother and son from such an early age? (Only cases teachers have observed were from already neurotic parents.)

Creativity? Machines? As in learning a language, basics come first, then we go on. Individuals vary greatly in the use they make of their native language. *Not every person who learns to speak English becomes a great poet!*

What is memory? (There were frequent comments about the children's fantastic memory.) What is involved here is very different from memorizing a page of printed music by playing it over and over, finally "memorizing" the sound of one's own playing! Presumably there are usually better-sounding models available than one's own attempts to struggle through a new piece?

Questions from a thoughtful participant:

Does today's public school system give structured self-discipline, or is this why we have so much failure today?

Is man basically lazy, has to be taught self-discipline? Can you effectively say "Do whatever you want," without first giving the tools of self-discipline?

Can every child be taught to lead a self-disciplined life, *if he has the chance?* (Time will vary, as in learning a language or violin.) *After the child has achieved self-discipline he can have the freedom to live in an unstructured system.*

General Procedures

Each step along the way is mastered before going on to the next step.

Other important factors: 1. *Listening* (*very* important) to recordings of the music well played, 2. memorization (one teacher: "I am now planning to do much more memorizing in my own teaching."), 3. frequent repetition of music already studied.

Much work done (even with advanced students) on *preparation* for playing. Preparation is needed before playing—note the bad example of the father who drove away before the car doors were closed. Baby fell out! *Prepare for each note.* Play—stop—think—play.

Much use made of preparatory coordination and concentration exercises without the violin. New rhythm and motion are taught first without the bow by shaking hands in rhythm and by words with same rhythmic pattern (better than just clapping rhythm).

Play with eyes closed, or with eyes concentrating on one point, such as bow-contact-point. "Violin and eyes do not look at audience." To correct wandering eyes, have child look down. Two children may face each other and play; the one who looks up first loses (class watches).

Take a breath as you get ready to play. Rise on toes to take preparatory breath.

Since we do not use formal, printed études, we must work out our own practice drills, and find new and interesting ones.

"Each phrase is a room in a house—play to show where a new room is, and what kind of room it is."

Academic teacher says you cannot teach a child something his body is not developmentally ready to do. Motor controls needed to start violin: press thumb against finger called for; button and unbutton; tap shoulder, nose, etc.; work zippers. Many children don't know parts of body. Three-year-olds have attention span of fifteen minutes. [Optimistic?—C.C.]

A student often works on piece A for refinement; piece B for learning notes; isolated techniques from piece C, coming next; and reviews older pieces, previously learned.

"If you're having trouble with a note out of tune, you're not singing hard enough in your head."

The teacher's primary job is teaching the child how to practice.

Performance over, students bow and say "hippopotamus" to themselves (or count 1-2-3), before coming back up from bow.

One teacher meets the parents four times before a child's first lesson, and teaches a class of children (perhaps six of various ages) two 45-minute periods per week.

Students beginning at fifth-grade level in one school situation do no note-reading until about February of the first year. Note-reading starts with what is heard, not seen. *Perpetual Motion* is a good piece to start reading and seeing patterns. "Children learn to read when they show a desire." "Perhaps Americans can develop a way to *sight-read* well by the Suzuki philosophy, to add to his way of producing a beautiful tone and technique." (Then "the page will sing to you the way the record does.")

Creativity—make up motives or compositions within the structure.

Backtrack—keep checking on the old as you add new concepts.

Introduce Bartok Duos, learned from record, toward the end of Suzuki Volume I, as an introduction to contemporary music.

Always play repeats—if you don't insist, you've lost another opportunity for repetition. Review, repeat, be satisfied with nothing but perfection.

Place violin case on something flat, with a back to it (e.g., a chair).

Small child may stand on raised platform (Japanese teachers are on their knees when teaching little children). "Teacher's position" is where child's violin points (or the teacher may sometimes play along directly behind the child).

Twinkle Variations are based on rhythms of *Bach Double* and *Vivaldi A minor:*

Teacher was effective with quiet, smiling manner; her violin proficiency and charm won the children immediately.

Suzuki students develop individual styles because (1) they are exposed to more than one rendition, (2) they are treated as individuals themselves.

P[6]—Preparatory Pause Practice Produces Perfect Performances.

Teacher must:

Win respect of parent

Develop relationship between parent and teacher

Develop relationship between parent and student

Develop relationship between teacher and student

If instruction starts in first grade, an orchestra is ready by fifth grade. Children have difficulty reading music and watching a conductor simultaneously. If some conducting is introduced early, the children will be accustomed to watching a conductor before starting reading and orchestra playing.

An advanced student is given a choice of ways of doing a passage, with explanation of the historical view.

"Disastrous skips are sometimes made, in the enthusiasm of the parent or teacher to have the child playing more and more literature."

Tuning

"Be a tuning fork"—sing A and wiggle arms above head.

Teacher plays first rhythm on open string. Then student plays it, and tells teacher what to do in tuning his string. (Or class tells what to do in tuning.) Teacher does fine tuning.

(Teacher plays A, at first)—"Reach in air to find A, put it in your ear, pull it out of your mouth (sing 'too' or 'la')—now play."

"Monitor" tuning. Tune one E string, then that child plays it continuously while teacher tunes others to it. At end, all are playing open E. Then another child serves as "monitor" for A string tuning, etc.

Later, class sings A, tunes; sings E, tunes, etc.

Teaching Techniques

"Fix me" game—teacher plays badly, has children correct faults.

"Copycats" game—"Do as I do" (imitate teacher).

Class rocks forward on left foot as the phrase builds, providing *a specific way to help build the phrase.*

Play standing on one leg (stork), swinging the other. Reverse. (Weight on left, swinging right, while playing is better.)

To get practice at a slow tempo, "Let's play we're *Myrtle the Turtle* and 100 years old." Mr. Suzuki, however, says "Play like a young man, not an old man" (slow and stiff).

"You decide what you are trying to say, then figure out how you can say it that way."

Teacher asks "Why?" about many things—tries to discover reasons. Students are taught to listen to themselves, and to be critical. Class is divided into two sections, to listen critically to each other.

"Cymbals"—make big, circular, upward-bound clapping motions in beginning to loosen shoulders. Clap on beats of *Variations*. Change tempo.

Answer questions while playing open-string rhythms.

Brevity—"1E," not "put your finger down on E string."

"If I didn't think you could do it, I wouldn't pester you."

Technique for practicing fast passages: Break into small units, play one unit *in tempo*—stop (holding position)—think of what's coming—then play next unit in tempo. In six-eight—3 notes, 6, 12, etc. Slow practice is good, but not the only method.

Techniques for class memorization (much more difficult in class than privately):

> Small sections of piece at a time.
> Analyze in every possible way.
> Play through slowly, then up to tempo. Turn away, play again.
> "Freeze" on a trouble spot, check each individual.
> Use overhead projector to control where each child is looking.
> Use chord organ to analyze tonality.
> Memorize advanced pieces *first day*, if possible.
> Teacher helps. Work to capacity.

Students *talk* top notes, then bottom notes.

Lie on back on floor and play first rhythm or later piece, if right shoulder is tight or forward. Press for memory. This helps relaxation, posture, and position of left arm. "Take violin to bed, and play in that position." Play *Lullaby* with soft introduction from violin of teacher.

Students jump up and down with stiff and bended knees to show the difference between straight and curved knuckles.

Jump out phrases and sing *Perpetual Motion*—0122 (forward), 1 (back), 233 (forward). May also use letter names.

Staff on floor—students jump on notes and say note names.

Square Dances may be done while playing *Song of the Wind, Lightly Row, Duck Duck Goose, Twinkle* (shake hands square dance), etc.

Two tempi are used in lessons—slow, and immediately fast.

On *climax tone* of phrase, have children rise on toes.

Ask class member to begin a piece. Leader and group should breathe together before starting.

Bow A and E in succession; children identify string being played. Children, with backs turned, identify strings played by teacher.

1. Play first rhythm with left arm hanging at side.
2. Play first rhythm on each tone of A scale.

For rhythm of *2nd Variation:*

1   2   3   4

Clap clap tap nose clap, while teacher or piano plays this *Variation.*

tap hips or
jump

Word rhythms: ♫♫ ♫ = "Matsumoto tempo," "Mississippi River" (or Mississippi "Hot Dog"), "Chitty chitty bang bang," "Johnny get a hair cut," "Rosin in the left hand," etc.

♫ ⅞ ♪♫ = "Robin, I'm Robin," "My name is Ruthie," etc.

"Hamburger" equals ♩♫   "Yes, Ma" equals ♩ ♪
etc.

Syllables: *"Taka taka tak tak"* is better than
            "Taka taka ta ka" or
            "Tete tete ta ta" or
            "Dada dada dum dum." The first gets a cleaner
            sound.

New piece: teacher plays, children imitate each phrase, stop.
Call out finger numbers: "E 1-2-3 down," etc.

"Make up-bow and down-bow equal in sound, as harmonica
on inhale and exhale."

Teacher forces children to *listen* and *think,* to react *quickly*
and stay *alert.*

On open strings of *Variations,* quickly shift hand up to third
or fourth position and back.

Teacher places excellent emphasis on phrasing and breathing.
"Crunched" tone is loud and scratchy at first, with small bow,
gradually lengthened and refined. *One factor only* stressed at
lesson.

Reading charts are good to use when working on reading.

"When work is extremely well planned and presented, children respond beautifully, and their improvement is marvelous to
hear."

Hold of Violin—Stance

"To pad or not to pad" makes no real difference—whatever is
best for the individual.

Use Dr. Scholl's bunion pads to make jaw comfortable on
chin rest.

"Let's introduce your chin to your shoulder. Hello there."

Count 1-2-3, quickly place chin on shoulder.

Count 1-2-3, quickly place legs apart.

Count 1-2-3, quickly do both the above at the same time.

Chin and shoulder together, violin is set in place. (Give new
students the violin from behind, so they won't "grab with chin.")

"Some people have a cold shoulder, cover it up, warm it up."
Children's violins then move around to better position.

"Heads up—avoid sleepy heads—don't sleep! Stand tall." *Head back* is a remedy for droopy violins.

Change from rest position to "hold violin" position as quickly as possible, at count. Race to pick up violins from floor to playing position, after count of three.

Check firmness of hold by tapping down on child's violin (held without hand), or by "Let's see if I can take your violin away"—pull on scroll.

Placement of feet: Apart (width of shoulders). Jump and put feet together, then apart, etc. Jump up in air, land with feet in playing position. Correct foot patterns may be traced on sheet of paper for individual student.

Push student to see if his stance is balanced.

Number 4 game to place violin: 1. Left hand holding shoulder of violin, hold arm's length in front of player; 2. point violin inward and up; 3. turn head to left shoulder; 4. place violin on shoulder and chin on chin rest.

Nose ("ski-jump," aimed towards strings, "so jumper won't fall to floor"), strings, left elbow and left foot all lined up makes good playing position. Fifteen-pound weight of head goes down on violin.

If violin sags, teacher holds his hand up to where violin should be. Child brings violin up to touch teacher's hand.

Holding violin in place without left hand—is the child able to talk? Shake left hands with partner? Hold gumdrop lightly between teeth? March as piano plays *Variations?* Swing arms, bend and turn?

Appoint an assistant to circulate in group to fix posture. "When you see him coming, fix yourself."

Cello shoulders and player's parallel. Check position by extending arms out on each side and holding cello with knees.

Numbers for cellist's posture: 1. Sit forward, with back and shoulders straight; 2. hold cello arm's length away; 3. spread feet; 4. draw cello in. For left hand: 1. Extend arm out to left; 2. place palm forward, with fingers forming a "C"; 3. bring forearm in to fingerboard; 4. place fingers on string.

Violin playing taught in this order: 1. How to hold violin, 2. how to hold bow, 3. how to move.

Small child may sit on teacher's knee and play—attentive and close.

Stop—hold left hand straight in front like traffic cop
Think—point to head with left hand
Play—place left arm in playing position

Left Hand, Wrist

Left hand is a "mirror"; if you can see yourself, then the wrist is ok.

"Traffic cop"—make stop signal, then shape hand for violin, keeping it flexible.

Don't let wrist "pancake."

For balky, collapsing left wrist, loop large rubber band over scroll, slip left hand through it.

Fingers of Left Hand

Shift hand along violin neck, swing elbow freely under violin, point first finger to ceiling, then fold it down in place.

Finger exercise—put down 1-2, then take off *quickly*

put down 1-2-3, then take off quickly, etc.

Use fingerboard tapes to fit major tetrachord pattern for beginning players.

"High and low" in fingering not clear on violin (and completely reversed on cello). Concept of second finger *touching* first is clearer to children at beginning than concept of second finger *low*.

1, 2, 3 down, then lift 1, 2 up. *Do not develop the "block fingering" habit,* use fingers one at a time. Block fingering is clumsy and does not clear the way for vibrato.

Exercises for finger quickness and strength: "crab pincher," with each finger opposing the thumb; snap thumb with each finger in turn, keeping circle. Pluck G string with left fourth finger (both directions). Competition in playing first two notes of Gossec *Gavotte* as many times as possible.

Fingers hover "like helicopters" over correct landing places. "Don't lift them up and throw them away." "Don't put fourth finger down in basement." With three fingers on, the fourth should be above the string, "waiting like a helicopter."

Play high 1-2, low 1-2. Increase speed. Then high 2-3, low 2-3, etc.

Fingers operate like little hammers—lift and set. Throw finger down, after bow-stop. Snap finger so you hear it hit the string.

Teacher plays out-of-tune pitch, child moves teacher's finger to correct it. Intonation check: Stop in middle of piece and check pitch of each child. "Do we sound like one violin?" Test for a child, listening in the hall: Is the teacher playing, or the class?

Teacher plays student's piece, but stops before every second finger note to have student move teacher's finger to correct place.

"First finger is *out of town*" (not in proper position).
"Second finger is *in the attic*" (straight up in the air).
"Third finger is *in the basement*" (under neck of violin).

Talk or sing through song with the fingering numbers.

Cello "target practice"—left arm down at side, quickly find finger's place on string on command. "A 1," "D 4," etc.

Violin g minor arpeggio—place third finger on g on D string, then *feel* with first finger on A string for B and B-flat.

Trills: "touch hot iron" etc. Backwards: "lift second finger quickly to see if there is a flea under it, but don't let him out."

Shifting preparation: Siren's wailing—slide finger on string. Practice 1 2 3 4 patterns in second and third positions on all strings.

Fiocco *Allegro* is the big left-hand technique piece. Get it up to tempo!

Hold of Bow—Exercises

Flutter middle finger against bent thumb. Make circle with right thumb and each finger in turn, bringing them together rapidly in "snapper" fashion. "Make a bunny" with right hand; *chin* on bunny assures bent thumb.

Shake out hands; after count "1-2-3," bring thumb and second finger together. Look through "telescope."

Pick up pencil with second finger and thumb, many times. Pick up dice with two fingers. Use pencil to practice moving hand in first rhythms of *Variations.*

Pick up bow in middle with left hand, place right fingers on bow. Tip of bow, held in middle by teacher, placed on student's left shoulder—student's right hand falls into place for good bow hold. Knuckles face toward *tip* of bow.

Horizontal bow (tip held with left hand)—tap various right-hand fingers on bow twenty times. Emphasize "springy knuckles." Point bow to ceiling, tap curved pinky.

Bow hair placed on teacher's finger to add weight from "100 to 500 pounds." Student takes hold of teacher's finger like bow-stick to show power. Suzuki always works from strength and power, "strong, but relaxed."

"Spider crawl"—fingers walk up and down bow-stick, held vertically. Game: Who can finish trip first?

Student holds bow in vertical position or on string; teacher taps stick to see if bow snaps back quickly.

Control bow with *bent thumb* and *pull* on second finger.

Practice with first finger off the bow—then work for more power.

Fingers = boxes, filled with weights, on bow.

Cello—everything "leans in" toward cello, including back of bow hand.

Vertical bow—swish bow, keeping tip straight. "Make wind with bow." "Windshield wiper" (two kinds)—wave bow back and forth. "Rocket blast-off," after countdown, from floor to ceiling (exercise for control of *tip* of bow).

Grip frog tightly, then relax. Relax pinky at frog, so tip is *heavy.*

Practice various motions while holding bow in air, at "nine o'clock, three o'clock," etc.

For work on bowing directions, students bend knees and

move body up and down, corresponding to direction of bow stroke.

"Elevator"—bow held horizontally; "move people up and down on it." Keep bow steady, ↔ and ↕

Cello—aim bow through a "ring of fire" made with left hand. Keep bow in tunnel, made by fingers.

Look at "wristwatch" on right arm. Hold the inside of right elbow with left-hand fingertips, bow rhythms (as teacher plays). Have students stand back to back, right elbows together.

Practice bow movements of piece with bow held vertically in air, as teacher plays (pantomime). Check hand placement. Teacher pantomimes bowing of piece in air—class identifies. (Or teacher claps rhythm, or knocks it on back of violin.) Class pantomimes teacher's touching bow to string in various parts.

Lift and set bow repeatedly (helicopter fashion) on E string, on A string. Set bow, at part called for, on string called for.

For long up-bow, "Can you touch your nose?" (with tip of bow). Then set bow on string and start. For long down-bow, lift bow hand to nose, touch string and start at frog. Continue down-bow to floor. Repeat.

Hold bow by tip, reversed, then exercise and play, to get feel of more weight.

Draw a phrase in the air with bow arm. Discuss phrase ending.

Developing Use of Bow

Teacher to class: "You be *echo* to me." For solid tone, play loud enough to "make echo." Pluck D string, send sound to ceiling—listen for echo—let sound roll around—then match with bowed D. Starting at tip, play swift up-bow stroke, let bow come off, listen to echo. Faster the bow, longer the echo.

Practice up-bow with breathing in and shifting weight to left foot, going up on right toe, or swinging right leg in air. For freedom, practice whole bow up on an eighth note—*throw* the arm. Inhale on up-bow, exhale on down-bow—step to left, step to right, swing free leg. Or, on down-bow, bend knees and feel weight of arm. Send body weight up with up-bow. Drop elbow on down-bow to give relaxed bow arm.

Find maximum tone and use it on fast tones as well as slow. "Press tone," with little bow, is taught and tolerated at first—can lighten up later. Maximum tone is always emphasized. Practice some without first finger on bow—for big sound—apply weight through middle of hand, not just first finger. Use longer bows to get louder sound. Change dynamics by amount of bow used, at first. Exaggerate dynamics.

Strong tone—what causes the bow to lose pressure? Students' answers: Changing strings. Vibrato shakes bow off. Fingering. Too wide motion of bow.

Lifting-elbow motion is important in lower half of bow. "Elbow plays the violin." Right elbow and hand are kept at the same height. Elbow movement should be taught gradually and early. (Later, the elbow and wrist are treated as *hinges*.) A pillbox may be placed on the wrist to develop elbow motion in the lower half of the bow.

Tape may be placed between F-holes on top of the violin as guide for straight bow. Make bow a "telescope" or "gun"—teacher looks through from frog to point, to keep it aimed right all the time. "Freeze" means stop and check positions—is bow straight? Straight stroke practice: Teacher places bow on string at tip, student slides fingers up and down on stick, getting feel of straight line. Frog-middle-tip game: teacher straightens bow at each stop. Teacher holds a pencil at left side of instrument, to impede bow from slipping over fingerboard. Straight bowing is a matter of "feel." Students must learn to move by feel, like a blind person. Place bow at frog, then at tip, quickly, several times before playing, to feel the straight line the bow should travel.

Tighten hair so there is "a child's finger-space between string and stick." Tape "boundaries" on middle section of bow-stick, or mark bow-stick's divisions with chalk.

Place rosin box on back of hand, with bow horizontal. Move in air and balance box on hand or wrist.

Avoid a sound like wind rushing through tree branches.

Bow to get a "long arch" sound in phrasing.

Many exercises should be bowed on open strings with the left arm hanging at side.

In *détaché,* upper arm should be slightly involved for improved resonance and singing quality.

Child is constantly trained to have quick responses in bowing and everything else. The bow is a "sports car" or "jet plane" that moves fast in advanced playing.

Stress *quick* lift of bow in *Song of the Wind.* Develop circular motion on successive down-bows, listen to echo. Echo each phrase (f-p). "Offenbach"= successive down-bows, lifting and returning bow to frog.

Play *Twinkle* at tip-frog, alternating.

Play *Twinkle,* alternating tones with circles in air.

Teacher plays "Old MacDonald," children join on open E string at right time for ♫♫ ♪ , or ♫ ♫ , etc.

Imitate teacher's ⊓ & ∨ on open string, varying speed. Watch teacher's bow-tip as guide.

Following teacher, bend, bow, squat, etc., while playing rhythms on open strings.

"Don't break the magic spell of the last note"—bow stays *on* string a bit, at quiet ending of a piece.

Avoid last-note "hangover"—everyone stop with bows in air, then start again on new phrase. Also, this is a good way to silence a group before starting.

Practice *Humoresque* off-string at frog.

Perpetual Motion in sixteenths— ⊓∨ "one motion." Practice on open string, then play piece slowly, with silent stop after each ⊓∨ stroke.

Children pair off and shake left hands while bowing first rhythm continuously on one string (or bowing rhythms played on piano).

Staccato = "diving into the string." Place bow and bend knees to develop staccato. Teach piece first semi-staccato; then teach musicality and expression. Two basic bowings—*porté* (rhythmic) and *chanté* (singing).

Vivaldi *Concerto in A minor*—practice pizzicato to develop

clear sound, then trill each note ♪| ♫♫ . (Such procedures

should develop sharper bowing.)

Advanced students work on beginning pieces to play with longer bows and achieve higher ability. Relearn staccato pieces, now playing legato.

Tonalization is like polishing a table: "Really *rub in* that polish!"

At phrase-endings, bow "takes off like jet plane," continuing past the strings. Later, keep the bow on, but imitate the sound.

Early 1972, when this chapter was being put together, brought several significant developments in the Suzuki movement in America:

1. In February the Eastman School of Music of the University of Rochester held a four-day Symposium on Music Teaching and Learning, of international scope and significance. The climax of this affair came on Saturday evening, February 12, at a special convocation to award an honorary Doctor of Music degree to Shinichi Suzuki. Dr. Suzuki was brought from Japan for the occasion and delivered an address, "The Law of Ability." President Robert Sproull of the University of Rochester presided.

2. The publication by Summy-Birchard Company of *Suzuki in the String Class* by Paul Zahtilla, a beginning class method (with recording) for all string instruments. This long-awaited work, which has Dr. Suzuki's blessing, is intended for public school classes where *all* the string instruments are needed to form orchestras. The writer used this material in his own classes years ago, made suggestions for improvements, and served as consultant.

It is a distinct personal pleasure to note these two events in the first quarter of 1972.

Roger North (1650-1734), in his pamphlet *The Musicall Grammarian*, writes of the state of music in England during the latter half of the seventeenth century: ". . . for many chose rather to fiddle at home than to go out and be knocked on the head abroad." In the United States during the latter half of the twentieth century Mr. North's statement is apropos. Unfortunately, an American who "enjoys fiddling at home" may also be "knocked on the head abroad," as shown by the tragic experience of Robert Rimer, former Director of Music for the Cleveland Public Schools, who was robbed and severely beaten while driving home after an evening All-City High School Orchestra rehearsal.

Suzuki attempts to improve both phases of the situation described by North. First, by enabling more people to play the strings pleasurably at home or elsewhere. Second, by attempting to produce *better* people, less likely to be head-knockers.

Both are worthy aims!

Address to Second American Suzuki Institute
(Wisconsin State University, Stevens Point, August 7, 1972)
Clifford Cook, Oberlin, Ohio

Greetings—and welcome to the second American Suzuki Institute. The success of the first one, held here last year, may be measured in part by the registration for this year, about doubled. We all hope and expect that the present Institute will show a gain in *quality* equal to the great increase in *quantity*. This will provide a worthy aim for all of us this week.

First, let me bring up to date several of the points made in my talk at the opening of last year's Institute. In answer to the question "How many geniuses has your Talent Education turned out?", some now seem to be appearing. Apparently many of our Suzuki programs are getting beyond the steps involved in holding violin and bow (although I am still pondering the question posed to me by a child here last year "Do you know the number eight game?"—and if anyone comes up with a numbers game exceeding my ten fingers, I'm sunk!).

A twelve-year-old girl, Lilit Gampel, recently soloed in the Bruch *Concerto in G minor* at a New York Philharmonic Promenade Concert, conducted by André Kostelanetz. In his very favorable review in the magazine *Saturday Review*, July 1, 1972, Irving Kolodin writes ". . . her talent was uncovered through the (mass) method of training devised by the Japanese pedagogue Shinichi Suzuki. Score one, then, for the Suzuki method."

Dylana Jenson, an eleven-year-old Californian, has already made more than a dozen solo appearances with orchestras. She began her study at age four with the Suzuki method.

Between the East and West Coasts, much notable Suzuki playing has been done—a young girl, Kim Reeves, playing a Mozart concerto with Chicago's Grant Park Symphony, a youngster winning a scholarship to the Galamian Summer Camp at Meadowmount, an eleven-year-old boy assistant concertmaster of a university symphony orchestra, a high school sophomore playing professionally in a high-class summer music theater—plus the hundreds of other examples the present audience could add. In view of all these minor miracles, when I think back to my own start on the violin, in the eighth grade and with *Hohmann Book I* on the stand before me, I can only exclaim "What wonders hath God wrought!"

It is a pleasure to report that, following the criticism of my Suzuki book in *The Strad* magazine, the concerts of last October by the touring Japanese children, given in London's Queen Elizabeth Hall, evoked rave reviews in London newspapers, reading strangely like what the Strad called my "rather nauseating gush about the marvellous results of the system."

One more carryover from last year: While change goes on constantly, not all changes are necessarily improvements. For example, the now common practice of adding a perfunctory second part to all the Suzuki pieces from the very beginning is *not* an improvement, in my opinion. When the first appearance of a second part came with *Perpetual Motion* (an *effective* second part, by the way), it added something agreeably new in Suzuki study.

Another example: When my granddaughter obviously did not know the sound of a spot in the second violin solo part of the Bach *Double*, I asked, "Aren't you listening to the record?"

"Yes." So I listened to her record of Volume IV, heard the version with a string orchestra chugging along merrily—and *I couldn't hear anything of her part at the spot in question!* (I then mentally took away a little of the blame which I had previously placed on the "in-law" side of her heritage.)

Now let us come up to date with the topic for today:

1972, The Age of Youth

Ours is a youth-oriented society. This is nothing really new—Ponce de Leon sought to establish one a long time ago, but he discovered Florida instead. A certain thirty-four-year-old college president now considers forty the age at which one "goes over the hill," and acts accordingly. He stresses the need for frequent rejuvenation of his "back forty" faculty, and they emphasize his need for "maturation." I'll be curious to know his ideas seven years from now!

Fifty-five was already the retirement age in Japan some years ago. Sylvia Porter recently headed a column "Who cares about the elderly?" Today the top brass of the Westinghouse Electric Corporation are to be "semiretired" at sixty, "to enable younger men to get to the top sooner." There is even a school of thought which favors starting young people at the top, then letting them work down to their appropriate level.

Sibelius was often criticized for about thirty unproductive years at the end of his life. Perhaps he merely showed unusually good critical judgment, sometimes lacking in those of advanced years? In forestry, removing the older trees which have passed their prime and replacing them through natural regeneration, or by planting or artificial seeding, improves the health and growth of the forest.

In 1957 I wrote in a book: "A curse to be avoided like the plague is a group of power-loving officers who seek to become a self-perpetuating board." (The National Association of Schools of Music had, for years, such a board.) It is a pleasure to report that there are changes in the Talent Education Board, name, and organizational setup—which will be announced later. More changes will occur soon, and there are now some *ageless* women on the board. Young blood is still badly needed, however, in all phases of our common work.

Cute pictures of tiny young violinists in newspapers and magazines now often feature one-year-olds playing. Fortunately, judging by the form shown, we do not hear the sounds they produce. This emphasis on the ever-earlier start reminds me of the time I had Mr. Suzuki give a short "lesson" to two unborn babies. While I thought it a good idea, a friend said it was *"fetal."* Zoltán Kodály, asked when a child's musical education should begin, replied: "With the selection of its grandparents!" Years ago (P.S.—Pre-Suzuki) I was somewhat puzzled by Robert Shaw's suggestive use of the term *pizzicato milkbottles.* Now I understand; it refers to pizzicato practice (both right and left hand) which a baby should do while supporting his nursing bottle. Natural-feeding mothers, however, may not favor excessive pizzicato practice! A whole school of boxers is developing, in which the youngsters eat a box lunch first, then play the box. Let's hope there is no Boxer Rebellion!

We cannot avoid the subject of The Generation Gap or Rock of Ages (referring not to an acid "rock" group or combo, but to the swing of the pendulum from the old Oriental veneration for age—the Geritol set—to the American lack of respect for it in the "Crunchberry set"). We are in the midst of many battles between change or innovation versus "The Establishment." There is no need to point out to you the conflict between many traditionally trained musicians and those who espouse Mr. Suzuki's ideas! There are frequent embarrassments arising from little children playing better than much older ones, older children having to play little children's pieces, Japanese children playing better than those one has taught by another method, confrontation with the possibility that one has been wrong all one's life! The child's learning from what we *do*, not what we *say* (as shown by a child's answers to questions about a stoplight: "Red means stop! Green means go! Yellow means *go faster!*") The generation gap between what Suzuki children *play* and what they *read*. All these points are in addition to the normal "generation gap" in its usual meaning.

An issue of the Oberlin Alumni Magazine contained a photograph of Professor Margery V. Aber teaching a Suzuki class of children with her violin balanced on top of her head. Someone asked what she was doing; my reply—"Using her head!"

Unfortunately, the belief is rather common that the only way many virtuoso violinists use their heads is *to hold the violin in place.* (This has also been said of Suzuki players.) I have read that an adult head weighs about fifteen pounds (mine will not unscrew so I can weigh it separately; some "friends" suggest I take reducing pills for mine) which provides the weight to hold a violin securely *under* the head in the normal position. *Hair!* (attached to the head, not to the bow) adds to the weight available to hold the violin in place. Thus, a long-hair hippy may have several pounds more weight to apply to a violin chin rest than did Mischa Elman (or several of us on the faculty). In fact, today's youth revolution in long hair is simply returning to the style of the romantic violinists—Paganini, Joachim, Ysäye, Ole Bull (the Norwegian violinist, not the Spanish matador, *Olé Bull!*), etc. Professor Josef Gingold says he doesn't mind his violin students looking like Wieniawski, providing they *sound* like him, too! Personally, I'm more interested in what's *inside* a head than outside.

The younger generation today is much interested in *ecology:* "the science of the relationship between organisms and their environment." We here well know that Suzuki Talent Education has for many years been vitally interested in the relationship of very young children to their environment, and in clearing up the *sound pollution* which has long been considered inevitable in the early stages of violin study! Even in the more advanced stages, Mr. Suzuki's strictures against "the press tone" may eliminate a question cellist George Neikrug once asked a conservatory sophomore, after her jury exam in violin: "How often do you have your bow rewooded?" Talent Education may also be able to obliterate the popular image of Nero, and to elevate the dictionary definition of *"To fiddle:* to make aimless movements, as with the hands. To trifle. To waste time."

Now a few thoughts for the various segments involved at Stevens Point this week. First, for all the adults: It sometimes seems to me that a problem of Talent Education in the States is that there are too many Chiefs and not enough Indians. Very appropriate to the present time is the definition of a politician as "the weathervane type of leader who sees which way the crowd is going, then runs to get out in front."

Even in our affluent society, the prices sometimes charged for lessons, and the teacher's rakeoff on sale of instruments in some locations, etc., suggest that "golddigging" plays some part in Talent Education in the States, as it does in Japan. I remember that on my first visit to Matsumoto, an American woman missionary there advised me "If you want to succeed with this movement in America, give women something about which they can stick up their noses!" (I trust she was *wrong.*)

One of the worst statements I have ever heard about a teacher was this: "She has high ideals for other people!" All of us need to review from time to time the ultimate goal of Talent Education, dealing wth its uplifting effect upon us as human beings.

When a friend once pointed out to the venerable Dr. Johnson, at a violin recital, how *difficult* the instrument is to play, the good doctor's reply was "Difficult? I wish it were *impossible.*" This is a frequent problem in music today; so much playing says only "See how well I do this," but says *nothing* that concerns the listener. Consequently, there are never enough paying listeners, and cynical statements are common, such as "Music schools are training people for unemployment." (The cover picture on the 1971 annual report of the Ohio Arts Council, entitled "Arts in Austerity," shows a violinist playing, clad only in a *barrel.*) But today, as always, *when music comes from the heart, it goes to the heart.* Nothing is said about how good the playing is, or anything else, but tears come to the listeners' eyes!

Some facts about the touring Japanese children should be made known to Americans, so that we do not delude ourselves too much, feel too inferior and inadequate, or get the impression that the Japanese children can play with one arm tied behind their back and after just a little fun practice when they have nothing else to do. Referring to two of the leading performers in the tours through the years: One practiced about five hours a day long before she started to school; another did not attend public school, but tutored privately so she could practice on her violin more hours per day.

Isaac Stern says that when he plays, his mind covers the past, present, and future—what he has already played, is playing at the moment, and is about to play. "*Music in essence is what happens in between the printed notes, not on the notes themselves,*" he says. This sounds familiar to Suzuki-ites.

A pearl is produced only when an *irritant* works on an oyster. Perhaps some irritation is necessary to produce a musical pearl? *(Parents please note.)*

Several thoughts for teachers:

Many roads lead to Rome, but *some do not!* There are about as many varieties of Suzuki in the States as there are of religions and subdivisions thereof (probably to be expected in the kind of ethnic melting pot we have in our country). Many Suzuki programs in the States are at the crossroads today. Where do we go from here? It is obvious that ensemble and orchestral training experience are much more important here than in Japan. Maybe the best way to learn to read music is to *start reading music* at the appropriate time, with blackboard and theory courses incidental? Perhaps someone here today can do for sight-reading what Mr. Suzuki has done for the basics of violin playing!

A final question for teachers to ponder (after two little ones from Yvonne Tait's beginning Suzuki Class cried because they missed *Dr.* Cook's session—easy to correct): How many of our students have cried *after study* because they *had* to come?

For the *children:* A bird at Louisville practiced one piece ("Bob White!") from morning until night every day for a week—he developed a beautiful, clear tone! (I told him he could go on to the next piece the following week.) At Blossom Center a few nights ago, a whippoorwill in the woods nearby added his song to the *Alpine Symphony* of Richard Strauss which the Cleveland Orchestra was playing. An attendant went out to find the bird and stop his song. Children, when you sing on your violins you should be *en*couraged, not *dis*couraged. And you should practice well *every day* to develop a beautiful, clear tone on every piece you play! (Fathers: the 3 most neglected men in the world— 1. Whistler's *father* 2. *Grandpa Moses* 3. *Lord* Godiva! When an Italian said to a friend "Your wife is a beautiful swimmer" the reply was "When we met, she was a street-walker in Venice.") Practice, practice, *practice!*

Shinichi Suzuki has a rare ability to treat the most serious matters in a light, humorous way which still contains more than a little truth. For example, Mr. Starr reports that when Mrs. Suzuki and some Talent Education leaders once asked Mr. Suzuki what they should do when the time came that he was no longer present to lead them, his reply was: *"Go skiing!"*

Let us not be "plus royaliste que le roi"—more kingly than the king, more pious than the pope, more saintly than the saint. Let's have a fine time together this week!

Chapter IV

Fritz Kreisler

In late January, 1962, when Fritz Kreisler died less than a week from his eighty-seventh birthday, the musical world gave full expression to a universal feeling of sorrow at the passing of a great violinist and a great man. There is no need to summarize the outpouring of messages, editorials, and biographical stories which his death brought forth. The facts of his life are common knowledge and he was admired and beloved the world over. All an individual can do is to pay his own personal tribute.

My first hearing of Kreisler's violin "off the record" came when I was a young schoolboy, after a trip on an interurban streetcar from Crestline to Cleveland, Ohio. The concert was held in the old Masonic Hall on Euclid Avenue. When Kreisler walked on the stage, I thought "This is *somebody*." For the first time, I saw the coat lapel pulled back and the violin tucked in place. I remember thinking that his bowing was a bit rough for the first two or three minutes; I did not yet know that it was his custom to "warm up" on stage. Then—what tone, what rhythm, what personality! As the program of Bach, Handel, Grieg, Bruch, and the final group of short pieces unfolded, a young boy was completely captivated with all he heard and saw; a lifelong attachment had begun.

From that Cleveland concert until Kreisler's last concert in Carnegie Hall, November 1, 1947, I do not believe Kreisler ever played within one hundred miles of where I was located that I did not go to hear him. Oberlin, Chicago, New York, San Antonio, Birmingham (where, in performing his edition of the first movement of the Tchaikovsky *Concerto,* he played in the cadenza a harmonic so pure and lovely that the sound stayed in my mind for days—one of the most perfect sounds I have ever heard).

I have no idea how many times or where I heard him in recital or with orchestra. Once in Chicago, my ear was glued to the keyhole in the door of Leon Sametini's studio while Kreisler played for "Sam" privately, as many artists did.

I never shared Olin Downes' perturbation when he discovered that the *Prelude and Allegro* was composed by Kreisler and not Pugnani. It is a fine, effective number for violin, and Kreisler's only motive in ascribing some of his own short compositions to others derived from his innate modesty. This music is marked "In the style of——" (not *by*——). And though I had to admit that his critics were right during a later period when his playing was out of tune and below par, I felt correctly that this was a temporary "slip." Even during that period, I felt that his playing offered something that was missing in the performance of many "correct" violinists. Call it "heart, feeling, warmth"—whatever you prefer; with Kreisler it was *always* there. And his tone was always the kind that made Karl Gehrkens say he enjoyed hearing Kreisler tune his violin.

Kreisler's playing of his *Liebesfreud* (love's joy), *Liebesleid* (love's sorrow), or *Caprice Viennois* (Viennese caprice) all went straight to the heart. Kreisler was a violinist who could *communicate*. How can music *by* and *for* computers communicate to the human heart?

In Fritz Kreisler's final concert in Carnegie Hall at the age of seventy-two he played Bach, Schumann, Chausson, and a group of six of his own compositions or arrangements. (I still have a cover from the extinct magazine, *Coronet*, which shows a portly mother admonishing her young son, who dangles a cheap violin case behind him, while they look at a poster of Kreisler playing— in front of *Carnegie Hall*.)

Here are two short quotes from R.P.'s review of the recital in the *New York Times*, November 2, 1947:

> One of the great secrets of his appeal has always been that, as well as being able to meet the masters on equal terms, Mr. Kreisler, perhaps more than any other famous virtuoso, has always been able to play with unwavering sincerity the sort of pieces that ordinary people love to hear. . . .
> The audience showed it could have gone on listening for

much longer, applauding for three minutes after the house lights
had been turned up. "He's a wonderful old man," one woman was
heard to murmur. Everyone seemed to feel the same way. . . .

My own notes on this recital read:

> Audience stood when he came out. Same tone, style, and
> stage presence as always. Some out of tune, but what of it? Liked
> the audience (full house) at this concert—many kids with their
> parents, old folks, musicians, every kind but much nicer than
> the people at most concerts in New York, it seemed to me. Stage
> lights had to be turned out to get people to leave at the end.
> What a man! Something sad about this—these two old white-
> haired fellows (Carl Lamson was the pianist) pull at the heart-
> strings as they stand and bow, hand in hand. More than one
> moist eye when they played *The Old Refrain* for an encore—
> perhaps because others thinking the same as I, that one of these
> days this golden tone will be silent, and there will be a gap in
> music which no one else can quite fill.

Several radio appearances on the Bell Telephone Hour, the
last in 1950, completed the long list of live Kreisler performances.
On his eightieth birthday, in 1955, he spoke on a network program in honor of the occasion. Once more the modest, generous,
warmhearted Kreisler was in evidence, through his voice this
time. (Casals' motto applied equally to Kreisler: *Everything
from the heart.*)

Time soon brings changes. In November of 1960 I read in our
college paper a review of an artist's cello recital, written by a
college sophomore, which prompted this response in the *Oberlin
Review:*

Reviewer's Reference to Kreisler Puzzles Cook

To the Editor:
    I am puzzled by one part of the review of Joseph Schuster's
recital, written by _____: "here his characteristic restraint and
good taste kept the music from degenerating into a Fritz Kreisler-
type of performance." Perhaps _____ was present at Kreisler's
farewell concert in Carnegie Hall in 1947; it was an experience
I remember with much pleasure. But surely _____ was not
older than seven when he then heard Kreisler for the last time?

Fritz Kreisler's peak performances were given before _____ was born, yet they are treasured in memory and missed by many musicians and music lovers today. Old recordings may have helped _____ form his judgment, as machines now dominate the musical lives of many youngsters. If this is true, _____, why did you waste so much time listening to those old recordings of degenerate Kreisler performances of Mozart, Beethoven and Brahms concerti?—*Clifford Cook*

There was no reply from the youthful critic.

After Kreisler's death in early 1962, *Caprice Viennois* was played many times as a tribute. Some of these performances turned out to be even more of a tribute than was intended. For example, one young violinist on TV did a good, clean job; he played the notes in tune, but the piece didn't turn out to be *Caprice Viennois*. Erica Morini happened to be playing in Oberlin at the time. Her performance came closest to Kreisler's own style of all those I heard—perhaps because she too is Viennese?

Kreisler's recordings have for years provided the examples of tone emphasized by the well-known Japanese violin teacher Shinichi Suzuki. I have enjoyed hearing young Japanese violinists play Kreisler pieces in true Kreisler style. The master lives on!

Kreisler had a sense of humor and loved a joke as well as anyone. There are many stories. Mischa Elman once asked Kreisler, during a train trip together, what violinist had the greatest influence on him. Kreisler at once named Wieniawski and became so eloquent on the subject of the beauty of his playing that both Kreisler and Elman were practically in tears. It was not until Elman reached his apartment in New York and looked up more information on the great Pole that he discovered Wieniawski had died when Kreisler was four!

Nothing has been said in this chapter about Kreisler's vibrato, his very personal bowing style, his fingerings, etc.—these have been thoroughly discussed in many books and articles. Let me close with this simple statement: Though I had the opportunity of speaking only a few words with him during his life, when I read that Fritz Kreisler was dead, I felt that I had lost a dear friend of long standing.

Chapter V

String Festivals

(The first of seven Oberlin College-Community String Festivals was described in detail in Chapter XII, "Multiple-Part Music for Strings," in my book *String Teaching and Some Related Topics*, published by the American String Teachers Association in 1957. For any readers who have not seen that chapter, most of it is reproduced here. Those who have read it can skip to "Second Festival.")

Multiple-Part Music for Strings

The possibilities for combining players of different proficiencies are numerous and encouraging. Less advanced students gain inspiration and ideals of tone and technique from playing with more skilled performers. The teacher or conductor must be careful that the overall sound of such a mixed group is good enough that it will not make the experience irritating to the better players. If this condition is met, only good can come from combining players of various levels.

There is nothing new about the principle of multiple-part music. Many examples might be given; let us consider only two. The Haydn piano trios have cello parts which are much easier than the piano and violin parts. And in the Haydn string quartets the first violin part is often much more difficult than the other three parts.

How can this principle be applied to combining strings in a Christmas concert? If we arrange "Silent Night" in D, for example, beginners can play open-string parts throughout. The regular parts can be played in first position by players at this stage in their study; the piano or organ may be needed to fill out the sound. More advanced players may play, in positions and with vibrato, the regular parts an octave higher. A still more advanced violinist (or group of violinists) may play a high descant. In this way players of several levels may be combined into a rich and full-sounding ensemble. Of course a balance must be maintained among the parts, but beginners do not get as much tone as more advanced players and so a considerable number of beginners may be used without their sound standing out too much.

Another example of multiple-part music for strings is the *Open String Concerto* by Ving Merlin (Boston: B. F. Wood). Of the string orchestra parts, violins A, B, and C are fairly difficult. Violin II and viola are rather easy. Cello and bass parts require some position experience. There is a piano accompaniment. The solo violin part (which may be played by a group of violinists) is for open strings, but calls for some spiccato, col legno, and four-string bowing with "open bow" as well as open strings!

In carrying the multiple-part principle to its logical conclusion, Ralph Vaughan Williams has written a fine *Concerto Grosso for String Orchestra* (Oxford University Press) which points the way. This concerto is written for four complete string sections, each playing parts of a different level of difficulty. The concertino parts are fairly difficult, while the tutti parts do not go above third position but contain some simple double-stops. One of the Ad Lib. orchestras plays in the first position; the other is limited to open strings. Thus the range is from advanced players down to beginners.

The concerto is in five movements with playing time about seventeen minutes. Despite the limitations which the composer placed on himself, the work does not sound "written down" or condescending. It is a valid, musically worthwhile expression of Vaughan Williams. The writer is enthusiastic about this composition and what it can do to help the string situation. Why can't more composers give us genuinely musical pieces which will excite the youngsters and amateurs and give them the thrill of playing along with the "pros" in a happy mixture?

College-Community String Festival

What can be done to promote and publicize the strings? How can youngsters who have already started their study be inspired to continue and to improve their playing? What can be done for players after their schooldays are over? How can music help to unify some of the different groups in a community? As one possible answer to these questions, the Oberlin Conservatory of Music sponsored a College-Community String Festival on December 10, 1955.

The evening concert began with Corelli's *Christmas Concerto*, played by the string section of the Oberlin Orchestra, David R. Robertson, conductor, with the concertino parts played by Constance Field and Larrie Moore Howard, violins, and Peter Howard, cello. Next, Haydn's "Lark" Quartet was played by the Oberlin String Quartet, Andor Toth and Elaine Lee, violins, Larrie Howard, viola, and John Frazer, cello. The finale was R. Vaughan Williams' *Concerto Grosso for String Orchestra* (1950), performed by 177 players from conservatory, college, public schools and town (Oberlin's population is about six thousand). This Festival String Orchestra was organized and conducted by the writer. It consisted of 100 violins, 27 violas, 34 cellos, and 16 string basses. At the same hour as this concert, a Gilbert and Sullivan production with full orchestra was being given in another auditorium in Oberlin. Various reasons prevented other string players from taking part in the festival; if it had been possible to assemble them all at the same time, about 250 might have played—where to put them would have been a major problem, as may be seen by looking at the cover picture!

During the Corelli and Haydn, those players taking part only in the Vaughan Williams sat in side balconies, directly above the performers. Rapt expressions on the faces of young string students testified to the effect of hearing fine performances by advanced and professional players. But actually participating oneself is even more exciting!

MULTIPLE-PART PERSONNEL

Ages of players ranged from eight to about sixty. Housewives, a dairy farmer, faculty members and students of Oberlin College and Conservatory, public school children from fourth grade through high school—they were all giving their best toward a common goal, and having a good time in the process! Many family groups of from two to four members played in the festival. David Robertson, Director of Oberlin Conservatory, played violin; one of his young daughters played violin, the other played cello. Wesley Smith and Arthur Williams of the Music Education Staff played open-string violin parts; Dr. Smith's young daughter played first violin. Wolfgang Stechow, Professor of Fine Arts, played viola; his young daughter played cello. Clyde Holbrook, Professor of Religion, played cello while his wife played viola; their son played violin and their daughter played viola. And so it went!

MULTIPLE-PART RESULTS

Organizing, editing parts, scheduling and conducting rehearsals, arranging seating and staging, plus many more details add up to a big job for someone. But the excitement and thrill of the youngsters, the pleasure of adult players who have no regular performing outlet for their talents, the appreciation of parents and others in the audience, the feeling of unity in a most unusual conglomeration of players engaged in a worthwhile project—these are some of the rewards for the work involved! Yes, the College-Community String Festival is one answer to the questions raised earlier in this chapter.

Second Festival

The next in our series of College-Community String Festivals occurred on January 5, 1957, and followed the general pattern previously established. The Vivaldi-Nachez *Concerto in A minor,* for two violins and string orchestra, was played by Professors Andor Toth and Matthew Raimondi with the string section of the

Oberlin Orchestra, David R. Robertson, conductor. Then came the Popper *Requiem,* Opus 66, for three violoncelli and orchestra, with soloists Peter Brown, Caroline Arnold, and Frank Church with the Oberlin Orchestra under Director Robertson.

The large Festival String Orchestra of 177 players, conducted by the writer, then gave the first performance, in manuscript, of Paul O. Steg's *Concertino Piccolo,* composed especially for this festival. Mr. Steg, then assistant to the director of the conservatory, wrote the five movements to accommodate any and all string players, including an open string violin part. This worthwhile composition was well received by players and audience alike; it was later published by Skidmore Music Company, Inc., of New York and has been widely performed. Not as difficult as the Vaughan Williams *Concerto Grosso,* it is well written for the strings, effective, and very useful. It has been a pleasure to conduct many times; the printed small scores have been helpful, as well as the regular-size full score.

Third Festival

For the third Oberlin College-Community String Festival we faced the problem of new repertoire for our large string orchestra with players of several different levels of proficiency. It was too soon to repeat either of the works played in the first and second Festivals; several composers had expressed interest in writing something for us, but none had produced a new work.

The writer recalled a *Concerto Grosso for String Orchestra and Piano Obbligato* by Ernest Bloch, written while Bloch was director of the Cleveland Institute of Music and published in 1925.

Note: Critic Robert Finn wrote in the Cleveland *Plain Dealer* for May 20, 1966, as part of an interview with Suzanne Bloch, the composer's daughter:

> Ernest Bloch would compose at night and on Sundays, returning to his office to work on Sunday because, in his words, "there is nothing better than a music school with no music in it."

When he saw his pupils here treating conventional tonality and form as old-fashioned, Miss Bloch said, her father determined to show them that adherence to these values could still produce exciting music.

"He wrote a 'Prelude' for piano with orchestra. We all helped copy parts and took it down the next day for the school orchestra to try. Everybody loved it and there was great excitement. So he added other movements. This became his Concerto Grosso."

This work is today perhaps Bloch's most widely performed piece. Suzanne Bloch remembers her father saying, "It is not, of course, an important work, but I think schools will like to play it."

The Institute Orchestra performed this composition under André de Ribaupierre in the summer of 1926, when the writer was a student member. A strong and original work, it seemed a good possibility for festival use, with the addition of some easier parts to the printed ones. These easier parts would consist of Violin A (first position), Violin B (open strings), Viola A (first position), Cello A (mostly first position, a few spots going to third), and Bass A (mostly half and first position, a few spots going to fourth).

Here are a few quotes from correspondence on this project:

Donald F. Malin, then President of C. C. Birchard Co. (now Summy-Birchard Company): "We are rather dubious about the possibility of obtaining Mr. Bloch's consent to another edition of this work. He usually prefers to have them appear as he originally published them."

In February, 1957, the writer requested permission from Mr. Bloch to add simplified parts to "a work which I consider the finest American string orchestra composition of the twentieth century and which would be very effective when played by our large group of strings."

In March he replied: "I would not be opposed to your proposal if the publisher is consentant, also. But I am somewhat doubtful about the results. It might be for you to decide after trying. It seems, also, that with 150 players and even more, *one single piano would be out-balanced*, and you ought to have several of them." (This was proven not true—with 181 players.)

By the end of the summer I had scored simplified parts for the Prelude, Dirge, and Fugue movements. The third movement, Pastorale and Rustic Dances, was omitted as it would not arrange effectively.

The Third College-Community String Festival was held on January 11, 1958. The program included the Brahms *Quartet in C minor*, Opus 51, No. 1, played by the Oberlin String Quartet: Andor Toth, Matthew Raimondi, William Berman, and John Frazer; the Mozart *Sinfonia Concertante* in E-flat Major for violin, viola, and orchestra, with Professors Toth and Berman as soloists with the Oberlin Orchestra; and, finally, the Bloch *Concerto Grosso* with Professor David Moyer, piano, and the Festival String Orchestra, conducted by the "arranger." The orchestra included 105 violins, 29 violas, 30 violoncellos, and 17 double basses. As always, its membership ranged from grade-school beginners to adult professionals.

A tape and program were sent to Mr. Bloch. On January 24th he replied:

> I am *very much* touched by your so kind letter and thank you heartily for it. If I were in better shape I would write you at length. . . . but I am a very sick man, perhaps near the end. Since months, I *escaped* from a Portland Hospital, 2 weeks ago, in order to complete a work here; the Doctors were ready to *mutilate* me, in a horrible way, even with *no certitude* about a cancer. . . . I am resigned to my fate, if it has to be, but not yet hopeless.
>
> Thanks again and to all those who took part in the performance.
>
> Cordially yours
> ERNEST BLOCH

Mr. Bloch died on July 5, 1959.

Fourth Festival

This was held on January 10, 1959. Mr. Bain Murray, acting music critic for the Cleveland *Plain Dealer* at the time, wrote this review for his paper:

Oberlin Innovation
String Festival Unites Expert With Beginner

Broad waves of Vaughan Williams' spirited modal polyphony rolled out of Oberlin College's Finney Chapel last Saturday night when Clifford Cook led 163 string players, aged eight to sixty, in a sonorous performance of the late (d. 1958) English composer's Concerto Grosso for String Orchestra.

This "do-it-yourself" project brought together violinists, violists, cellists, and double bass players from the fourth grade through high school, the college, faculty and town, to participate in Oberlin's fourth Annual College-Community String Festival.

Cook had organized his diversified crew of housewives, students, faculty members, a dairy farmer, and other townspeople, into groups based on ability, rather than on age. The stage was crowded. Older players on beginning parts sat next to school youngsters, giving them self-confidence. Rehearsals had been kept at a minimum, although younger players had studied their music for some time.

Ingeniously scored with four varying levels of difficulty, the Vaughan Williams work (1950) found Oberlin Orchestra students fiddling the more challenging Concertino part, while beginners played the easy parts in first position and on the open strings.

The group gave this massive, hearty Concerto a lively, spirited performance. The tough-fibered orchestral lines were well-etched and surprisingly in tune, with the open string parts blanketing the musical landscape like English mist.

Cook, who is Associate Professor of Strings and Music Education at Oberlin Conservatory, first thought of building a string festival in 1955, when he realized how many string players lived in Oberlin (population with students is around 7,800). Cook has found in the past few years that these festivals increase interest in string music, bring together many different groups of the community, and inspire youngsters to practice harder.

Good Experience

It is an invaluable experience for young beginners to play in an orchestra and to hear and help create a real orchestral tone. Cook feels there is a place for beginners "all the way from open strings up to the most difficult part they can play."

The three earlier festivals, which each had around 180 players, featured the Vaughan Williams work, Bloch's Concerto Grosso for String Orchestra with Piano Obbligato (Cook arranged easier parts for beginners), and Paul Steg's Concertino Piccolo for String Orchestra. This year, Steg is supervising the studies of Oberlin

Conservatory's Junior Class at the Mozarteum in Salzburg, Austria.

Earlier on Saturday's program, gifted young cellist Peter Howard skillfully brought out the deep color of Fauré's melancholy "Elegie for Violoncello and Orchestra." Howard, a Conservatory Instructor, was quietly accompanied by the Oberlin Orchestra led by Assistant Director James S. Ballinger.

The Oberlin High School Girls' Chorus and String Orchestra opened the program with six French folksongs, arranged by Franz Bornschein, led by public school music directors Harold Peterson and Douglas Handyside. The entire festival was cordially received by the audience.

Cook has reason to be enthusiastic over the success of these string festivals. He encourages other groups to plan them. The Vaughan Williams work has been performed in Dallas by the symphony orchestra and school youngsters, he said.

Cook feels that string festivals may be given any place where there is a strong core orchestra to absorb the raw sounds of beginning string players. And, we may add, where there is a musical leader enterprising enough to organize such a large-scale community project.

Fifth Festival

The Fifth Festival was held in February of 1961. The program opened with Haydn's "Sunrise" Quartet in B-flat Major (Opus 76, No. 4), played by the Oberlin String Quartet: John Dalley, Larrie Howard, William Berman, and Peter Howard. The Festival String Orchestra of 158 players then gave its second performance of Paul Steg's *Concertino Piccolo,* this time from printed parts (Skidmore Music Co., Inc.)

The final composition was the writer's *Suite 16 for String Orchestra,* given its first performance. The four movements were:

Tuning Prelude
Pickin' on the Pentatonic
Very Free Fugue (on a ribald theme) for Three Vices
Variations on "Cabbage"
    Theme
    Sauerkraut
    With Corned Beef

Kohlrabbi
Le Chouchou
Chinese
Old King Kohl
What! Again?

The program notes for this work read as follows:

Suite 16 was written in July of 1960 to add a light touch to
the repertoire for string festivals. Its parts range from moderate
difficulty down to an open-string violin part.

Tuning Prelude checks the open strings of all instruments and
their harmonics, as well as featuring bits of repertoire for each
instrument. This movement should appeal to listeners who
prefer preconcert sessions to the concerts themselves.

The second momevent is largely pizzicato, most of it based
on the open-string five-tone scale of C D E G A. Little pentatonic snatches of various tunes are combined into a kind of quod-
libet (or at least a potpourri.) The original waltz in the middle
is built on the pentatonic scale of the black keys of the piano.
The last section returns to the white key pentatonic, completing
the integration of this movement.

The third movement is a product of the composer's early
(swaddling) period. It was written when he was studying at
Chautauqua in the summer. One evening his roommate went to
the movie, leaving the moneyless composer in his room with
nothing to do. For this fugal composition we are indebted to the
inspiration of sheer boredom!

The Variations comprising the finale of the *Suite* probably
speak (some may prefer "smell") for themselves. In self-defense,
the composer can only say that since he has written a book which
his friends promptly labeled *The Cookbook* with great hilarity,
it is perhaps only natural that the present opus should close with
a vegetable movement showing some acquaintance with culinary
treatment!

The *Tuning Prelude* has been published by Mills Music, Inc.
(now Belwin-Mills), but at the current rate it will be the year
2000 before the entire work is published.

After this Festival, Marion Bradley Kelly wrote in her column
in the *Oberlin News-Tribune* "There is something about grown-
ups from the town and faculty, students and children playing

together that hardly can be resisted. . . ." The writer feels this is true, and has no regrets for the hundreds of hours he invested in the Oberlin College-Community String Festivals.

Sixth Festival

The unique feature of the Sixth Festival, January 16, 1965, was that it marked the first appearance on a Festival of 30 young violinists from the Oberlin Suzuki Class of about 45, taught by the Misses Hiroko Yamada and Hiroko Toba. The youngest child was three years old. With Marsha Kindall at the piano, the children played seven pieces from Suzuki Volume I, ranging from *Perpetual Motion* to the *Twinkle Variations*.

The Boccherini *Quartet in A Major*, Op. 33, No. 6, was then performed by the Oberlin String Quartet: Stuart Canin and David Cerone, violins, William Berman, viola, and Mary Fraley Johnson, cello. This performance was quite an "eye-opener" or "ear-opener" for the little children who had just played.

The Festival String Orchestra of 136, with Dean Norman Lloyd at the piano and the writer conducting, then played the three movements of Bloch's *Concerto Grosso* which we had first done in the 1958 Festival. The program noted "Our performance of his *Dirge* we dedicate to the memory of a full-blooded musician who contributed most generously of himself to the art he loved passionately." (I believe the young players who took part in, or listened to, this performance of the Bloch *Concerto* sensed that "something special was going on." At least, I hope so!)

Characteristically, Dean Lloyd thanked the writer for "letting him play piano," and on February 1 returned to New York City, to become the first Director of the Arts Program for the Rockefeller Foundation.

Seventh Festival

The finale in our festival series was held on December 10, 1966, exactly eleven years after the first one. As in the first, the Vaughan Williams Concerto was played, for the third time, by about one hundred and twenty-five players. This composition still gave the conductor a thrill. Professor Thomas Cramer asked me after the concert, "Did you ever hear the sound of the Festival Orchestra from the rear balcony? [I hadn't] It's quite a sound!"

The last half of the concert was played by about seventy of our Suzuki children, taught by Eiko Suzuki, Kazuko Numanami, and Mrs. Bonnie Hudson, and with Mrs. Dorothy Mauney at the piano. They played thirteen selections, ranging from the Handel *Bourrée* and Brahms *Waltz* down to the first phrase of *Twinkle* (played by the two-and-a-half-year-olds). As I later listened to the tape, I heard, for the first time in our children's performance, some tone that reminded me of what I had heard in Japan!

It was appropriate that our series ended with the playing of young children, as they were much in my thoughts in planning for the first Festival. One of the greatest teachers of all time expressed it this way, "Suffer the little children to come unto me, for they are . . . ." If you want the truth, just ask a little child!

Addenda

String festivals similar to ours have been held in Akron, Ohio; Ithaca, New York; Dallas, Texas; and in many other locations throughout the United States. The English festivals have long been famous; the Vaughan Williams *Concerto Grosso* was written for one of these occasions.

Mr. Suzuki's annual General Concerts, given in Tokyo late in March, were national in scope and of course involved many more players than our local Oberlin Festivals. We were mutually ignorant of what was going on for some years, but a few interesting comparisons may be made:

Tokyo Festivals	*Oberlin Festivals*
First held in 1955.	First held in 1955.
No rehearsal together.	*One* combined rehearsal of one hour.
Almost entirely violin, a few on cello.	All four string instruments included.

Tokyo Festivals	Oberlin Festivals
Largely *solo* repertoire played in unison, sometimes with orchestra or band accompaniment.	String orchestra concerto grosso repertoire used for large group. String quartet or soloists with orchestra often included as *models.*
No printed music used—all playing from memory. *All* participate who wish to and are recommended by teachers—*encouragement.*	Orchestra music is *read* from parts. *All* play who want to and attend rehearsals—*encouragement.*

(Instead of drawing a small circle to *exclude,* a large circle is used to *include* practically all who really wish to play.)

The *most advanced* play along with beginners—*encouragement* and *inspiration* for the less advanced.	The same.
Size and *mixture* of group are impressive.	The same, although we included *adults* of any age, not just children and young teen-agers.
Musical, not just *massive.*	The same.

Some later compositions have been written for string festival use. There is a *Prelude for Massed String Orchestra* by Karl Kroeger (for four string orchestras), a part of the Contemporary Music Project Library, available through the Music Educators National Conference. And Vaclav Nelhybel wrote a *Danza for String Orchestra* for the twenty-fifth Anniversary String Festival held at Manchester College, Indiana, in April of 1971 (available from Joseph Boonin, Inc., 831 Main St., Hackensack, N.J. 07601).

Some of the problems involved in multiple-part festivals, as described in this chapter, are: 1. repertoire, already considered; 2. most advanced players—the experience must not be boring or irritating to the professional, or he will not play; 3. young, inexperienced players—their experience must not be traumatic or humiliating, or string promotion will go into reverse; 4. the festival must offer something worthwhile for the large majority of players in between the two extremes listed above; 5. the time element, very important for such a mixture of players of all ages, each with a complicated schedule of his own; 6. organization and realization of what seems like innumerable details (I often thought of a word from the text of the Beethoven Ninth Symphony: *"millionen!"*).

A complete consideration of Preparation for Festivals would make a book in itself. Only a few details will be mentioned now. Booking Finney Chapel for a complete Saturday (setup in morning, rehearsal in afternoon, and concert in evening, followed by cleanup on Sunday morning) and looking for a date when not more than a dozen other public college and town affairs would be scheduled in our little hamlet—early summer was the time for such matters.

Summer was the time for preparing the music. In the case of the Bloch *Concerto*, for example, the five easier parts I arranged in such a way that the score for them would coincide exactly, by page and measure, with the published score of the printed parts. My friend Gerald Humel, then a student-composer at Oberlin whose manuscripts have always been models of clarity, finished the master parts by October. They were sent to Rochester Photo Copy for duplication, and were on sale at cost at the Co-op Book Store well before our first rehearsal date. (Printed parts were also on sale for players not in the regular orchestras; members of regular orchestras used printed music bought by their sponsoring institutions. The Book Store obligingly kept records of the names of all players purchasing parts, and the parts they bought, so that I would have this information.)

Very careful editing of scores and parts has long been a *sine qua non* for the writer, so of course it was applied to our festival music. The less rehearsal time and the more players coming together from different "locations," the more important such editing is in securing a unified performance without wasting time. My markings were copied in duplicate parts by students in my conservatory string classes, for whom this was a good experience to have—at least, they knew the difference between the down-bow sign and the heel mark used in organ music!

Some study of the life and works of Ralph Vaughan Williams

paid off for the conductor. Williams once said to an orchestral player who questioned a note in his part: "It looks wrong and it sounds wrong, but it's right." This was to become my conclusion about a C# in the viola part, three measures from the end of the Intrada movement of the *Concerto Grosso.*

Students in public school string classes and in conservatory string classes would start working on their festival parts several months before the affair was to take place. To accustom them to the sound of the advanced parts we used a commercial recording (such as the Kubelik-Chicago Symphony record of the Bloch), the piano version of the Vaughan Williams, or a specially prepared tape of the *Suite 16.* Playing tests on memorized difficult spots from each movement of the Festival Concerto were quite effective ways of killing two birds. We called these "Spottsies."

About six weeks before festival time we sent out newspaper publicity on details of the upcoming festival concert and an invitation for interested players not already in orchestras or classes to contact me for registration. At the same time, we mailed out information sheets and registration cards to all community players known to us. Here is an example of the sheet and card for one year:

Dear String Player:

You are cordially invited to participate in the Seventh Oberlin College-Community String Festival scheduled for Saturday night, December 10, in Finney Chapel. We hope you will play in one selection on this program.

R. Vaughan Williams' *Concerto Grosso for String Orchestra* will be played by a large group composed of teachers and students from the College and Conservatory, and players from the Oberlin community and public schools. We have played this work successfully at two previous Festivals.

The string sections of the regular Conservatory orchestras play the most difficult parts. There are other parts of various levels of difficulty for all string players—Tutti parts of medium difficulty and easier Ad Lib parts—and all players are welcome. The music is on sale at the Co-op Book Store. Some of you may still have your parts from a previous performance.

This project will not require a lot of your time. Players not in regular Conservatory orchestras are asked to attend at least *two* of four rehearsals to be held in the Orchestra Room (25) of the Conservatory on the following dates:

Saturday, November 19, at 2:30 P.M.
Saturday, December 3, at 11:00 A.M.
Monday, December 5, at 7:30 P.M.
Thursday, December 8, at 7:30 P.M.

A combined rehearsal required of all players will be held in Finney Chapel at 12:30 on Saturday, December 10, and the performance is at 7:30 that night.

We hope you can take part. We believe you will enjoy participation in this unique College-Community project, as many players have in past years. If you can join us, please fill out the enclosed card and return it to me by November 12. I shall be glad to consult with players about appropriate parts to buy. Thank you.

Clifford Cook, Chairman of
String Festival
Oberlin College Conservatory of Music

REGISTRATION CARD

Name _____

Address _____

Your instrument _____

Do you have this instrument? _____

Others in your family who will play:

Name   Instrument   Own?

Please return this card by November 12, indicating that you will play in the College-Community String Festival. Thank you.

Note that required attendance at only two of four scheduled rehearsals—on Saturdays and two evenings during the week—gives flexibility to meet busy individual schedules. Signatures on sheets at the close of each rehearsal provided the checklist of those players who had met attendance requirements. The dress rehearsal the day of the concert was the only one required of *all* players, and a seating chart plus the exact number of chairs and stands required provided an "instant check" of attendance at the final required one-hour rehearsal. Fortunately, attendance "requirements" proved unnecessary.

In passing, just a word about the item, "others in your family who will play," listed at the bottom of the registration card. Many families took part in our festivals; the Charles and Dorothy Meek family provided the most players with six members playing in one festival. These people were of such quality, the writer was content to know that "The Meek shall inherit the earth." It will be in good hands!

As the Festival date approached, the writer would rehearse the string sections of already functioning orchestras at their regular rehearsal times. Here is the schedule for the year we first played Bloch's *Concerto*:

Oberlin Orchestra (55 strings)—three times
Collegiate Symphony (33 strings)—four times
High School Orchestra (23 strings)—several times, but they also came to the four optional Saturday afternoon rehearsals held that year.

The 70 other players attended Saturday afternoon rehearsals. The number of players on each part in 1958 was as follows:

Violin I—30	Violin II—30	Violin A—35	Violin B—10
Viola—17	Viola A—12		
Cello—22	Cello A—8		
Bass—9	Bass A—8		

All Saturday morning (the Festival day) we worked on setting up Finney Chapel. By 1965 the College Buildings and

Grounds Department had produced the setup plan shown on page 87.

They also brought about 100 stands, 10 Conservatory basses, etc., from the "Con" to the Chapel, and moved 165 chairs up from the Chapel basement.

Meanwhile, some student-volunteers and the conductor were transporting some 30 Conservatory violins, violas, and cellos, electric tuner, extra strings, rosin, music folders, signs, etc. to the Chapel. While the piano tuner worked on the grand to be used in the Bloch, we quietly numbered the stands with chalk, and placed them (with correct music folders in place) and the chairs according to my master plan. The basement rooms under the stage were labeled by signs to show the sections assigned to players of the different parts, and the Conservatory-owned instruments were all in place, having been previously assigned by number to the specific players who would use them.

Each player was assigned to a stand number and chair or position (34L, 60R, etc.), and a chart showing the numbering of the rows of stands, plus the personnel list with the assigned number by each name, was placed on a stand at each entrance to the stage area of the Chapel. All of this detail work was done to avoid having *one big mess* when so many players came together for a single one-hour rehearsal and one-hour concert. It was a lot of work, but it paid off.

Of course, the proven most effective placement of the different sections was used, and careful seating plans were made to insure that young, inexperienced players would have standpartners they could rely on and follow, such as Conservatory students who were just learning to play a string instrument, but were already good musicians in other areas.

The constant "A" from an electric tuner could be heard throughout the Chapel basement for some time before the rehearsal or concert performance of the *Concerto Grosso* started. Conservatory students were assigned to check carefully the tuning of all instruments played by children. When no "Tuning Concerto" was listed on the program, we didn't want one performed on stage; but accurate tuning is *very* important!

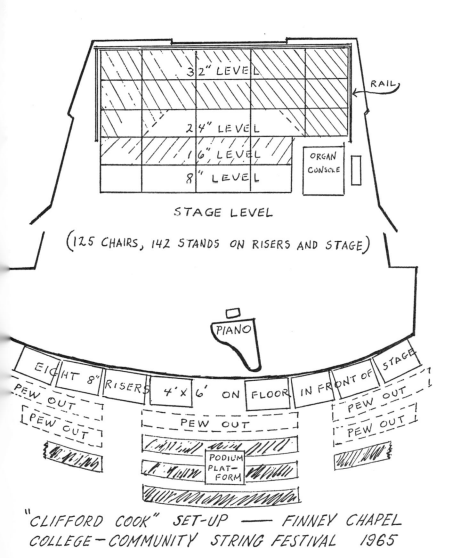

"CLIFFORD COOK" SET-UP —— FINNEY CHAPEL
COLLEGE—COMMUNITY STRING FESTIVAL 1965

We taped both the final rehearsal performance and the concert performance, to have two choices available. One year we put out a record of the Steg *Concertino Piccolo* and Cook *Suite 16.* Many pictures taken through the years provide a photographic record, and bring back vivid memories to the writer.

Enough of such details of organization. They have been stressed so much because *they are absolutely essential, if a Festival is to have a chance of being a smooth-running, enjoyable musical affair rather than a terrible time-wasting mess that turns everyone off!*

The thrill of the concert is reward enough. Afterward, it is pleasant to read a few words such as these in an editorial in *Triad* magazine for March, 1956:

> The feature of the program was the performance of R. Vaughan Williams' *Concerto Grosso for String Orchestra.* In writing of this performance in the Oberlin *News-Tribune,* no less a critic than Professor George Waln said, "The musical bigness, the richness of sound, the intonation—believe it or not—the fine precision in playing together came as an overwhelming surprise to this listener."
>
> Such an accomplishment requires some person of unusual organizing and musical ability. In these events, congratulations are due to Clifford Cook of the Oberlin Conservatory string faculty.

There were about 1,300 total participants in our seven String Festivals. The Festival String Orchestras included about 1,100 participants. Of these last, about 765 were different string players, many of whom played in more than one Festival. Appendix A lists the names of these players, with the Festivals each one played in.

Looking over this list of names of participants, the writer can visualize and recall most of them. A "mental file" contains facts (read or heard) about their lives since our paths crossed. *Interest in following the careers of students and friends in their later life provides one of the most pleasant facets in a lifetime of teaching and in retirement.*

Chapter VI

Interlude I: Conventions, or Ten Thousand Strong

(An address given at the Oberlin MENC Luncheon—Chicago, March 30, 1954)

The purpose of the first convention ever held was to raise Cain as well as Abel. This is still the purpose of most conventions.

Careful study of the many national associations which hold conventions may prove educational. For example, I once received a letter from a friend who casually mentioned that her husband was attending the Convention of the National Association of Parlor Tumblers, of which he was Secretary. This news intrigued me, as the gentleman in question was six feet tall and weighed over two hundred pounds. It was difficult to imagine him turning flip-flops from parlor davenports without disastrous results. Research showed, however, that this association was made up of breeders of a certain kind of pigeon. My background and tolerance have been broader since this exciting educational experience came my way.

My first convention was in Kansas City. The late Arnold Schoenberg gave the principal address at a general session; I read a paper at a small sectional meeting. Despite the discrepancy, I rather fancied the idea of twin-billing and stressed it to my friends. Here we find one good purpose for attending conventions. In Kansas City I became aware of the important extracurricular activity which goes with conventions—the socializing part—and learned Rule No. 1: Don't bring your wife. (At this point, attention was called to the presence at the Oberlin Luncheon of MR. Robertson, MR. Kennedy, MR. Waln, MR. Dominik, etc.)

In the heated congestion of travel to and from conventions

all sorts of contretemps occur, some of them providing topics of conversation good for years. Here is a newspaper clipping to show what I mean:

Suitcase Is Seldom, She No Fly, Plaint

WASHINGTON, D.C. (AP)—The AFL Air Line Pilots' Association said Thursday that a member it did not name reported that his company had received this note from a Japanese whose luggage was misplaced:

"Mr. Baggageman, United States of lax. Gentlemen, dear sir: "I dam seldom where suitcase are. She no fly. You no more fit to baggage master than for crying out loud. That all I hope. What the matter you?"

Don't you know just how he felt?

Chicago is a favorite location for conventions. In fact, so many conventions have been held there that Chicago is now widely known as the "Windy City." (Monday and Tuesday of the 1954 MENC Convention showed that there are natural as well as man-made reasons for the nickname.) There is, nevertheless, a certain charm about a convention held in some far-off, exotic spot; for example, the 1928 Convention of the Royal Geographic Society was held at the Royal Hawaiian Hotel in Honolulu. At this particular convention, the official word of greeting was, naturally, "Hawaii?" and the final word of farewell, "Abyssinia."

A good, snappy slogan crystallizes sentiment for any convention. This reminds me of a motto I happened to see on a wall banner in Fairchild House (a women's dormitory) in Oberlin: "When better women are made, Yale men will make them." Think of the rallying effect this motto would have at a reunion of Yale men! A motto which has always seemed to me to be apropos is that of the NPCMA Convention. This, of course, is the Convention of the National Potato Chip Manufacturers' Association, and their motto is "Let the chips fall where they may."

A prominent lady music educator has told me that a woman goes to a convention primarily to show off her new clothes. The general public holds firmly to the belief that teachers' conventions are mainly shopping expeditions for women teachers. I do not know that this is a fact, but I have noticed some correlation between the dates of a teachers' convention in a city and the appearance of a large amount of special advertising of women's apparel in the newspapers of that city.

The registration, badges, etc., the politics carried on in smoke-filled rooms—these and many other features are the same at all conventions. One suggestion for music teachers' conventions: when one of our young, ambitious, "get-ahead type" members, whose sole purpose in attending the convention is to look for a job, shows up at the registration desk, why not slip a "For Sale" or "For Rent" or "Available" sign around his neck? This would save much preliminary conversational sparring.

Convention programs generally come under one of the following headings:

1. Inspirational or "pointing-the-way" addresses. Many of these sermons aim at improving bad cases of erosion of the soul. Some of the addresses have as their *real* topic "How *I* Did It—Why Don't You At Least Try?" or, in the words of the Texan, "It Ain't Braggin' If Ya Done It."

2. Demonstrations or concerts in which we have the chance to hear many school music groups go through their daily routines (nothing especially prepared for the convention, of course). Seldom, thank God, do we hear the kind of performance depicted in Helen Hokinson's famous cartoon in the *New Yorker*. The chorus of the local women's club is in rehearsal formation; the director admonishes "And now, mezzos, let me hear the thunder of hoofs!"

3. Clinics in which we are shown by the paid judge how to correct it in ten easy steps.

4. Panel discussions. The principal speaker talks for the entire time, then the moderator says, "We're sorry there won't be time to hear from the panel, but thanks to you gentlemen for coming!" At many of these programs of all types there is splendid opportunity to observe pedaguese as she is spoke and wrote.

Then there are all sorts of small, informal affairs where good talk about music may be heard. For example, as you are coming down the hotel corridor, notice the small group of men with heads together, listening intently. Just as you get up to them, the speaker says the punch line, and they all roar and slap each other on the back. Obviously, this is enthusiastic talk about some musical subject. This talk goes on into the wee hours of the night. According to statistics kindly provided by The Simmons Company, "One third of your life is spent in bed." This fraction does *not* apply to the time spent at conventions.

A prime purpose for attending music conventions is to get acquainted with the latest materials available. I have found that the publishers' and exhibitors' parties are excellent places to sample their materials. When the representative of a leading publishing house says to you "Come up to Room 1243 around eight tonight"—go, you'll be sure to find his latest exciting materials on display. Test them for yourself.

By the way, excellent Bock Festivals are frequent after evening sessions, if the convention is held late enough in the spring.

In summing up, if we *must* make some slight criticism of most conventions—they're too *conventional!*

Chapter VII

Improving String Ensemble Repertoire

String players are fortunate to have a huge repertoire of ensemble masterpieces dating from Arcangelo Corelli (1653-1713) down to the present time. Many of these masterworks, however, require technical facility beyond that of most young players.

Suggestions

One way to improve the repertoire *performed* by younger players is to raise the level of playing proficiency so that the more difficult works of an excellent repertoire may be performed adequately. Hopefully, the early start in string playing characteristic of Suzuki and some other contemporary methods may lead to establishment of solid technique in many young players before they reach the "activities" stage, when they are pulled in so many different directions that real accomplishment in any field becomes difficult for them.

Another way to add to the quality of the repertoire most needed is to encourage *composers* (not educationist hacks) to write new ensemble works that stay within bounds technically. Obvious financial obstacles are involved for both composer and publisher. Commissions or prizes given by foundations, societies, and schools are of great value. The Ford Foundation project of placing young professionals as "composers in residence" in selected public school systems has been the most significant experiment ever attempted in this line. After many years of experience, evaluations of the Ford project are as varied as the individuals making them. One thing is certain—today there are many compositions in print and in use which would never have been written if it had not been for the Ford Foundation's project.

A final suggestion, most feasible to put to immediate use, is *to select better music from the vast repertoire already available for all levels*. In the exploring and sifting process there is always room for improvement, and this can be a rewarding and never-ending search!

Through the years the writer has found many sources for learning about and finding ensemble music for strings. Here are a few of them:

Sources

Chamber Music for Amateurs by John Hayward, *The Strad*, London, 1923. Of some value for materials suggestions.

Cyclopedic Survey of Chamber Music, compiled and edited by Walter W. Cobbett, 2 vols., Oxford University Press, 1929. The "Bible of String Chamber Music" for the period covered. Excludes music of the kind known as "teaching material." Contains many excellent articles on various phases of string ensemble repertoire and related topics.

Chamber Music in American Schools by Charles W. Hughes, Freybourg Printing Co., Mt. Vernon, N.Y., 1933. After much "busy" writing, the author finally gives good suggestions for string ensemble repertoire. (Unique work on ensembles in the schools.)

Kammer-Musik-Katalog by Wilhelm Altmann, Verlag von Carl Merseburger, Germany, first published 1910, later edition 1945. Published chamber music works since 1841. Large and useful catalog of all combinations with publishers listed. No commentary or evaluation.

Four publications of the American String Teachers Association, Urbana, Illinois:

Music for Strings, compiled by Frank Grant, 1953. Particularly good for English music.

Chamber Music for Strings, compiled by Angelo La Mariana, 1953. Works suitable for amateur performance.

List of String Duos, compiled by John Bryden, 1957.
Works *not* listed in Altmann's *Katalog.*
Materials for String Ensembles, compiled by Mary Sexton, 1962.
Result of much experience with children.
Interlochen List of Recommended Materials for Instrumental Ensembles (4th ed.), National Music Camp, Interlochen, Michigan, 1963.
Committee selections, graded.

Finally, four publications of the Music Educators National Conference, Washington, D.C.:

Materials for Miscellaneous Instrumental Ensembles, 1960.
NIMAC Selective Music Lists for Instrumental Ensembles, 1961.
Both the above are committee selections and graded. The first excludes music for the standard ensemble combinations.
Contemporary Music Project Library Catalog, vol. II, *Works for Orchestra and String Instruments.*
In addition to full orchestra and string orchestra, there are some chamber orchestra and smaller chamber works listed.
Selective Music Lists, 1972.
Solos and ensembles for like and mixed string, woodwind, brass, and percussion instruments, graded for difficulty. Compiled by NACWAPI and ASTA.

Complete editions of composers' works as found in large libraries are helpful in finding fresh music for string ensembles. There is valuable information in books on individual composers and their works, such as Marc Pincherle's *Corelli—His Life, His Music* and *Vivaldi—Genius of the Baroque,* Frank Howes' *The Music of Ralph Vaughan Williams,* and various books on Purcell, Handel, Haydn, Mozart, and many other composers.

The *Educational Music Bureau Guide to Materials* and the *Pepper Guide to Instrumental Music,* with their annual listings of ensemble music of different publishers, were helpful sources, as were magazine reviews of new music including ensembles for strings.

The catalog of the English *Polychordia String Library* has

long been of value. Other foreign collections should be mentioned, such as *Nagel's Musical Archives,* the Breitkopf and Härtel *Collegium Musicae Novae,* and the *Hortus Musicus* of more than two hundred publications. Catalogs of individual domestic publishers are too numerous to list here.

Music

The following are a few selected string ensemble suggestions, from duos through sextets. Most of them are playable by school ensembles.

Duos

2 Violins
Bartok, 44 Duos, B&H, II-IV
Beck (ed.), *Music for Two,* Mercury, III
Gearhart and Green, *Fiddle Sessions (Fun for 2, 3 and 4 violins),*
    Shawnee, I-III
Hindemith, *14 Easy Duets,* Schott (AMP), III
Pleyel, *6 Duets, Op. 8,* Schirmer, III
Prokofieff, *Sonata for Two Violins* (Difficult), International, V
Telemann, *6 Sonatas,* Mercury, IV

Violin and Viola
Beethoven, *3 Duets,* International, IV
Mozart, *12 Duets,* International, III
Mozart-Gingold-Katims, *2 Duets,* International, V
Whistler-Hummel, *String Companions* (2 vols.), Rubank, I-III

2 Violas
Rolla, *3 Duets,* Mercury, IV
Stamitz, *3 Duets, Schott* (AMP), IV

Violin and Cello
Bach, *4 Duets,* International, IV
Beethoven, *3 Duets,* International, IV

Glière, *8 Duets*, International, IV
Platti, *4 Ricercati*, Baerenreiter, III

Viola and Cello
Beethoven, *Duet Requiring Two Pairs of Spectacles*, International, V
Beethoven, *Minuetto* (from above work), Peters, III

2 Cellos
Offenbach, *6 Duos*, Schott (AMP), II

TRIOS

Trio Sonatas (2 Violins and Piano or Organ and Cello)
Corelli, *Trio Sonatas for Strings and Organ*, Mercury, III
Handel, *Sonata in G minor*, International, III
Handel, *Sonata in E*, Mercury, III
Mozart, *15 Organ Sonatas*, Mercury, IV
Purcell-Britten, *Golden Sonata*, B&H, III
Tartini, *Sonata in D major*, International, III
Die Hausmusikstunde (Vol. V), *Trio-sonaten & Stucke*, Peters, III

Concertos (2 Violins and Piano—or String Orchestra)
Bach, *Concerto in D minor*, Peters, V
Stoessel, Albert, *Suite Antique*, Schirmer, IV
Vivaldi-Nachez, *Concerto in A minor*, Schott (AMP), IV

2 Violins and Viola
Dvorak, *Terzetto*, International, V
Haydn, *12 Trios*, International, IV
Zimmerman (arr.), *Two Violins Plus One* (26 Trios—Viola or Cello), Schirmer, II-III

2 Violins and Cello
Beethoven, *6 Country Dances*, International, III
Boccherini, *2 Terzetti*, Mercury, IV
Haydn, *6 Trios*, Schott (AMP), IV
Mozart, *12 Minuets*, Schott (AMP), III

Violin, Viola, and Cello
Gibbons, *4 Fantasias,* Mercury, III
Hockner, *Das Streichtrio,* Simrock (AMP), III
Purcell, *3 Fantasias,* Mercury, III
Schubert, *Trio in B-flat,* International, V

Piano Trio (Violin, Cello, Piano)
Bach, *Jesu, Joy of Man's Desiring; Sheep May Safely Graze,*
   Oxford, III
Baron (arr.), *New Trio Album,* BMI, V
Haydn, *Trio No. 1 in G,* Boston, IV
Kreisler (arr.), *Trio Album,* Foley, IV
Mozart, *Trio No. 3 in E,* Schirmer, IV
Rissland (arr.), *20 Trios for Church or Concert Room,* Presser, IV

QUARTETS

2 Violins, Viola, and Cello
Dancla-Klotman, *Herald Quartet,* Mills, II
Hambourg, *Introduction to Chamber Music: No. 2, String Quartet in F,* Mills, III
Hindemith, *8 Pieces in the First Position,* Schott (AMP), III
Lockwood, *6 Serenades,* Mercury, IV
Mozart, *Quartets,* Vol. II, Peters, IV
Mozart, *Album of Easy Quartets (vol. II),* Kalmus, III
Pochon (arr.), *Flonzaley Quartet Favorite Encore Album* (No. 3), Fischer, IV
Das Streichquartett (2 vols.), Simrock (AMP), III
Purcell-Warlock-Mangeot, *Nine Four-Part Fantasias,* Schirmer, III
Sontag (ed.), *An Introduction to String Quartet Playing,* Fox, IV

3 Violins and Piano
Bornschein (arr.), *Easy Classics,* Boston, II
Gabrieli, *Sonata,* International, III
Vivaldi, *Concerto in F,* International, V

2 Violins, Cello, and Piano
Dvorak, *Bagatelles*, International, IV

4 Violins
McKay, *American Panorama*, Fischer, II
Telemann, *Concerto in D*, International, III

4 Cellos, 3 Cellos and Piano
Cheyette and Roberts (arr.), *4-Tone Folios* (3 vols.), Fischer, III
Popper, *Requiem*, International, V

Violin, Viola, Cello, and Piano
Loeillet, *Sonate à Quatre*, Elkan-Vogel, III
Lotti, *Sonata*, International, III

QUINTETS—SEXTETS

Dowland-Warlock, *Lachrimae or Seven Tears* (2 violins, viola, 2 cellos), Oxford, III

Heibert, Victor, *String Americana, Bk. II* (string quartet and piano), Witmark, III

Liepmann, *Popular Dances from the Seventeenth Century* (string quartet and bass), Boston, II

Mendelssohn, *Sextet, Op. 110* (piano, violin, 2 violas, cello, bass), Peters, IV

Purcell-Warlock-Mangeot, *Fantasia Upon One Note* (2 violins, 2 violas, cello), Schirmer, III

Telemann, *Concerto in G major* (4 violins and piano), International, III

Telemann, *Polnisches Konzert* (string quartet and piano), Hansen, III

Vivaldi, *Concerto* (4 violins and piano or string orchestra), Fischer, IV

Vivaldi-Ghedini, *3 Quartets* (string quartet with piano or organ), International, III

Watters and Pyle (arr.), *A Book of Violin Quartets* (with piano), Mills, II

Many varied, interesting, and instructive programs of string ensemble music may be compiled from the preceding brief lists. For example, here is a short program illustrating some contrapuntal devices:

For Two Violins
Telemann   *Sonata in Canon (Music for Two)*
Bartók   *Mosquito Dance* (No. 22 of *44 Duos*) (Canon written out)
Mozart   *Upside Down Duet (Fiddle Sessions)* (This one is sure-fire!)

For Four Violins
Haydn   *Minuet (Fiddle Sessions)* (Play to end, then backwards to beginning)

For Two Violins, Cello and Piano
Corelli   *Ciacona* (Opus 2, *Sonata No. 12,* International) (One of 48 trio sonatas by this composer)

Cello Teaching by Violinists

Traugott Rohner, former editor of the *Instrumentalist*, has written: "Some of the worst cellists are developed by violinists who think they know, but don't. Some horrible cellists I have judged at contests turned out to be pupils of violinists." A conservatory cello major supports Mr. Rohner's statement: "A violinist in public school music should be very careful in teaching cello. I was started on the cello by a violinist, and *it took me two years to undo what she had taught me.*"

Deplorable as this may be, the fact remains that in many school situations, if beginning cellists are not started by a violinist, they will not be started at all. What, then, are some of the basic playing differences between the two instruments which the violinist should know?

The weight of the cello rests on the floor, not on the player, adding resonance to the tone and making possible much more natural and normal use of the arms and hands than the contorted violin posture permits. The cello makes a "three-point landing" against the player, at the chest and the inner part of the knees—certainly a more favorable *locus operandi* than that provided by the violinist's method of holding his instrument between collarbone, neck, and jawbone.

Skipping the jokes about the cello's gender, we may note that the greater ease of holding this instrument is countered by the demand of its longer, thicker strings (especially the lower ones) for more strength and powerful action as well as flexibility and agility in fingers, hands, and arms. Development of larger "two-way stretch" in the left hand and early introduction of shifting are also called for in cello study, since the instrument is tuned

101

in fifths as is the violin, but its strings are very much longer than violin strings.

The fingers are usually at about right angles to the strings (left hand) and to the bow-stick (right hand). The little finger usually comes *over* the bow-stick instead of resting on top, violin fashion. The right thumb is used for pizzicato of chords and single tones at times. The fingers are often spaced farther apart than on the violin bow and the first finger has a big job to do in producing rich cello tone. The first finger balances the other three in cello bowing. It is often kept more separated from the others than is customary on the violin bow.

The left thumb is held *under* the neck and second finger, not at the side of the neck as is common on the violin. There is a larger open space between the palm of the hand and the neck of the instrument. The thumb is more free, may be removed from the neck at times during vibrato, and is also used as a stopping finger. The thumb register of the cello uses a technique entirely different from that of the violin's high register, with the thumb stopping two strings like a "movable nut."

Although the violin-type slant of fingers to string is used some on cello, the "squared" shape with fingers at about right angles to strings should be stressed. Using violin "shape" for the left hand on the cello simply will not work in most cases. More percussive finger action is used on cello than is usual on violin.

The hand span for cello normally covers a third. The minor third with small hand position—a half step between neighbor fingers—is not too much of a strain for most hands. But the major third—large or stretch position—begins to approximate tenths on the violin. Certainly the fingers must be trained to stretch apart more on the cello. Playing a whole step between first and second fingers calls for practice of two approaches to the extension: back with the first finger alone, and forward with thumb and all fingers but the first. Stretches may be practiced first in the fourth position, then brought down to the first. The fourth position is an important one on cello, corresponding somewhat in general usefulness to the third position on violin.

Cello vibrato is perhaps easier to initiate, since the left hand has no part to play in supporting the instrument. Cello vibrato uses more *forearm* motion than violin vibrato does. Use of the shifting motion of the forearm with a finger sliding on the string, then anchoring the finger while the forearm continues its motion is probably the most common approach to teaching cello vibrato.

In summary, most of the errors are due to violinists' trying to teach the cello as though it were a large violin—in every way except holding it under the chin! The single suggestion which will do most to correct the faults is to place the fingers at about a ninety-degree angle to the strings and to the bow-stick. This correction alone will go far toward silencing criticisms such as those quoted at the beginning of this chapter.

Chapter IX

Selection and Care of the Bow

While a satisfactory instrument is a basic requirement for progress in playing at *any* level, many experienced teachers feel that the quality of the bow is so fundamental it must come first. The finest performer cannot play well with a poor bow; he *can* play passably well on a true-proportioned, correctly adjusted instrument which sells far below the price of his concert Strad.

When the budget for an outfit is limited, get the best instrument possible, but don't skimp on the bow. A few extra dollars invested in the bow will pay worthwhile dividends.

Such matters as appropriate bow length and bow materials have been clearly presented in the MENC Minimum Standards. Of *first* importance in selection of a bow is the stick. If this is made of soft wood, it will soon "spring," warp, and lose its camber or inward curve, thereby becoming useless. Pernambuco wood, thoroughly seasoned, is a *must* for a really satisfactory stick.

The adequate bow will have a good "balanced feel" when held and manipulated. It will not be too quivery during long, slow strokes, yet it will give the player full cooperation in off-string bowings. Beware of a bow that forces the player to do *all* of the work!

Preferred bow weight is a personal matter which varies with different players. For class use, medium weight will be best.

If the wood of the stick contacts the hair during much of the stroke (with medium arm-weight applied) when the hair is tightened to one-quarter inch from the stick at the nearest point, the stick is too weak or the inward curve (camber) is too great. The sound of wood on the string is not pleasing, even in a professional symphony when the conductor drives his string section too hard. When purchasing a bow, check carefully the amount of weight needed to bring the stick down to the hair and string at the nearest point.

Sight down the length of the bow from frog to point. A new bow should be straight. A good old bow may show a slight curve to the left in the center. An unsatisfactory bow will curve decidedly to the right in the center. A very cheap and weak bow will soon develop excessive side-curve or twist.

Inexperienced players seem to have a mania for dropping bows; they have bad cases of "dropsy." Young bass players in particular enjoy dropping the bow on its point! Many instances of broken ivory at the point have caused the writer to favor metal there for the beginner. A well-seated ebony frog is also very desirable.

Beware of the carpenter-butcher who attempts to rehair bows; he can easily split and ruin a frog or, even worse, a tip. This is in addition to the usual crossed and loose hairs which make the poor rehair job a complete waste of money. A new bow should be equipped with high-grade hair that will tighten and loosen correctly, is rosined and ready for use.

The buyer should not have to rehair a new bow before he can use it. He should not have to replace the wrapping and leather of the fingergrip to make the bow usable. Yet many new bows will have tinsel, bone, or wire winding that skids around under the fingers and achieves the exact opposite of the purpose for which it is intended. Good quality wire, firmly wound and secured at both ends, with firm leather grip aiding the thumb at the frog end of the wire and leather ring securing the other end, provides needed finger and thumb support.

The bow screw should turn smoothly and easily; an occasional drop of oil helps. Hair length should be such that it can quickly be tightened to playing tension and relaxed when not in use. All too often one encounters sticking or slipping threads on bow screws and hair too short to relax or too long to tighten. Certainly none of these faults should be present on a new bow. Cheap bow screws soon "lose their heads" and must be replaced; better quality is a good investment in the long run.

In teaching care of the bow, here are some points to emphasize:

Handle it at the frog area only, *never* touch the hair.

Avoid dropping the bow or striking it against stand, chair,

etc. (For any youngsters who desire weapons for fencing provide good, sharp swords instead of bows!)

Never over-tighten the bow and *always* relax the tension on the stick when putting it away.

In the violin or viola case, always put the frog of the bow in the correct clasp, the tip in the proper slot, and face the hair in the right direction. Where cello and bass bows are kept on wall hangers, never hang a bow by its tip: use the stronger frog for this purpose. In cloth bags cello and bass bows should be placed frog first.

Use only a good grade of rosin, suited to the season. Some teachers apply rosin to the hair in one direction only. Don't thoughtlessly rosin a bow as a form of physical exercise—apply rosin only when needed and then in small amounts. Class bows tend to be over rosined; the "snowstorm" created by an excessively rosined bow occurs much too frequently. Perhaps the subtitle of this book would be better if changed to: Come, let us rosin together, but not too often or too much!

The underside of the stick should be wiped free of rosin daily. Much rosin here is proof that the wood is being ground down into the hair and string by excessive pressure or incorrect tension of the hair and stick.

Wipe the frog, thumb-, and finger-areas of the bow daily to remove perspiration soil.

Rehair bows frequently enough that the hair never develops the dirty, sticky look often seen. When the hair, properly rosined, no longer sets adequate strings into free vibration, it's time for a rehair job.

Following the MENC Minimum Standards and these few suggestions will do much to solve the bow problem. No discussion of bows would be complete without mention of a really excellent and comprehensive book, *Bows for Musical Instruments* by Joseph Roda, published by William Lewis and Son in 1959. (Paul Rolland visited Mr. Roda shortly before the latter's death, and described his visit in the *American String Teacher*.)

Chapter X

Reviewing Reviews

One of the pleasant privileges of being a string teacher comes to light occasionally when the local newspaper wants a review of a concert. Donning the robe of the "omniscient (?)" music critic, the writer offered the following three reviews in the *Oberlin News-Tribune:*

I. *Hungarian-Born Cellist Janos Starker Shows More Restraint Than Audience* [January, 1957]

The season's sixth Artist Recital was presented in Finney Chapel Tuesday evening by Janos Starker, Hungarian artist, who is at present principal cellist of the Chicago Symphony Orchestra, and soloist of wide experience, with Leon Pommers, pianist. Mr. Starker proved himself a serious, almost ascetic, musician with a well-disciplined technique always ready to meet the music's demands.

The opening *Sonata in G Minor* by Henry Eccles, an English violinist who became one of the celebrated Twenty-Four Violins of Louis XIV in Paris, is known in Oberlin, having been played here on violin, viola, cello and double bass. Mr. Starker played it in a straightforward, businesslike manner which announced at once that there would be no foolishness in his playing.

Bach's *Suite in D Minor* for cello alone received a clean, cool performance which suggested that additional poetry and deep feeling were being held in reserve. The artist's restraint and control were obviously appreciated by his audience

Next came the Hindemith *Sonata, Opus 11, No. 3* (written in 1922 when the composer was twenty-seven). In two main sections, this youthful Sonata exhibits some of the features Hindemith was to develop further, later in his career. There are kinetic figures, the busy work—the musical athlete keeps himself in trim with a good workout. The ostinato-like figures build to a loud climax, drop down and start the process over again. There are more romantic-sounding spots in this Sonata than in most of

Hindemith's later works. The "Pixy March" section is effective night-music with Prokofieffian touches here and there. The cute ending seemed unnecessary.

It was interesting to hear this composition played effectively by both artists with a kind of cool ardor. The audience liked it beyond doubt.

After intermission Beethoven's *Sonata in C Major* provided a quiet and contemplative interlude. Even in the quick sections there is frequent return to the reflective mood. Starker and Pommers caught and projected the spirit of this work admirably.

To close the program, Starker gave us another "a cappella" solo—the last movement of Zoltán Kodály's *Sonata* for cello alone. This provides the virtuoso a field day! Scordatura (bottom strings tuned down a half step) "slap" pizzicato with the left hand and strumming with the right (suggesting Spanish guitars no end), ponticello, tremolo slides in double stops, glissando pizzicato chords, harmonics—all the tricks are used to bring forth novel sounds from a solo cello and suggest Gypsy carrying-ons galore! The two Hungarians were exactly the right men to write and play this music which brought stomps and whistles of delight from the audience.

Starker's earlier restraint made his closing number all the more effective. The dazzling finale produced only one broken bow-hair; the cellist didn't even work up a good sweat in creating so much excitement!

Starker and Pommers made an effective team whenever they played together. Symmetry went as far as matching hairlines. There were very few times when the cello tone was covered.

For those who want something technical: the cello had a cork under the tailpiece—to kill a "wolf." The bow did not get hold of the string at times, making a little fuzz in the tone in some passage work.

The lone encore was Ravel's *Pièce en forme d'Habanera*. The audience wanted more, but once again Mr. Starker showed restraint by having the house lights turned up. A most enjoyable recital!

II. *"Old School" Quartet Pleases Reviewer* [March, 1959]

The current Budapest String Quartet, a veteran ensemble which has long held high rank in its profession, appeared on the Artist Recital Series in Finney Chapel Tuesday evening.

There were no novelties on the program or in the personnel of the quartet. The latter included Joseph Roisman and Alexander

Schneider, violins, Boris Kroyt, viola, and Mischa Schneider, violoncello. The program comprised Joseph Haydn's *Quartet in D Major, Opus 76, No. 5;* Ludwig van Beethoven's *Quartet in F Major, Opus 135;* and Robert Schumann's *Quartet in A Major, Opus 41, No. 3.*

No Monkeyshines

The platform demeanor of these four gentlemen of the old school proved pleasing to listeners who prefer to go to a zoo when they want to see monkeyshines.

This quartet does not scurry about the stage with Ferdinand-like pawings at the floor, as do some of the young quartets. They concern themselves with the music at hand and let it go at that.

Finney Not Ideal

Not much of the Haydn was needed to remind us once again that Finney Chapel is not an ideal hall for chamber music. Such a large, high auditorium leads players to force their tones, resulting in some rough, unpleasant sounds.

Balance is also a problem. The first violin tone was covered at times and the cello tone did not always come through.

Some of Mr. Roisman's top pitches did not ring the bell. Quartet intonation, as well as tone and balance, may suffer in too large a hall.

"Christmas Quartet"

This Haydn work is sometimes called the "Christmas Quartet" —though, like little Buttercup, "I could never tell why." Each of the first two movements is based on a single melody.

The second, the famous Largo in the unlikely key of F Sharp Major, is a favorite of many players and listeners. This beautiful singing movement was well played and cast its usual spell over the audience.

Everyone enjoyed a good cough when the music ended.

The Presto-Finale, in Haydn's insouciant, go-to-hell mood, was not turned into a race, for once! It had plenty of life, however, and was kept pretty clean.

Late Beethoven Tough

Late Beethoven is always a tough nut to crack. The Opus 135 received a considerable ovation from the audience. The first movement is Beethoven musing to himself.

The second movement is a grim Scherzo, without humor,

coming to a dramatic, soft ending. This movement was well played except for some high tones.

The Lento was sung convincingly, but a few bumps and slides were not too appropriate.

The last movement is something of an enigma. Called "The difficult resolution," the opening theme insistently puts the question "Must it be?"

Answer Comes

After a dramatic pause comes the affirmative answer "It must be!" The same process is repeated later in the movement. After a short pizzicato section (very effectively played) comes the final affirmation.

Written five months before Beethoven's death, the question and answer Finale does not sound to this listener like the musical joke some claim it to be.

At any rate, aside from some pitch trouble and rather dry tone, the Budapest Quartet proved their claim to laurels in this difficult music. The audience proved its claim if it really appreciated the music as much as its hands said it did!

Schumann Completes Program

The closing quartet was Schumann's last work of this kind, written in a few days of July, 1842.

Honestly romantic, full of falling fifths and rising fourths, this music was deeply felt by the performers. Violist Kroyt in particular took off his wraps and praised the Lord with a loud voice.

The Adagio movement worked up to the evening's climax as the entire quartet warmed to its task. Even the "snappy" (literally) Finale, with its charming Gavotte and Musette interludes and galloping climax at the end, could not match the searing romantic intensity of the slow movement.

Encore by Mendelssohn

An ovation from the large audience led to an encore, *Scherzo* by Mendelssohn. The elves were just a bit heavy-footed, but they did get around in a charming manner!

All-in-all, a very pleasant evening.

Some listeners prefer coming a little nearer our time than 1842. Perhaps the Budapest Quartet is a bit old-fashioned, not invariably in tune, the outside voices not always as clear or pleasant sounding as the inside ones (Put some of the blame on Finney Chapel).

Honored Musicians

These men are honored musicians who have served the Art of Music faithfully and with distinction for many years. They provided much enjoyment and satisfaction to this listener Tuesday evening.

Final recollection—President Stevenson, going out the chapel door, to Danny Born, custodian: "You played very well—one of your best concerts." Danny, smiling sweetly: "Thank you."

I believe they both liked the concert, too!

III. *Perfectionist Coaching Pays Off; Cleveland Orchestra Victorious in Opener* [October, 1960]

Under the lights of Finney Chapel Tuesday evening Coach George Szell gave his familiar signal for the kickoff in Oberlin's 1960-61 Artist Recital Series.

A platoon of string players promptly took the ball and marched and sang their way down the field through the four movements of Mozart's serenade, *Eine Kleine Nachtmusik.*

Led by their new captain, Rafael Druian, the string platoon showed deft and nimble fingerwork as well as considerable finesse with their bows. Carefully phrased themes were passed expertly from section to section.

If the first three movements were a bit chaste, the finale was a trifle chased in spots. The first quarter showed that this team, as usual, features a balanced attack, precision plays and split-second timing.

Enter Marching Band

The second quarter opened with a small marching band coming on the field for the first Oberlin playing of a *Concerto for Woodwinds, Harp and Orchestra* by Paul Hindemith.

The soloists were all effective in some deceptive end runs in the first two movements, but the trickiest play of the entire quarter was pulled by clarinetist Marcellus, who stood up and performed Mendelssohn's Wedding March while all sorts of feinting, short passes and runs went on around him.

This was probably the first time this particular play had been called in Finney Chapel since the Stevenson-Aluminum merger took place some years ago.

Most of the crowd recognized the tune, loved the horseplay and applauded lustily. (Composer Hindemith demonstrated his Teutonic thoroughness by telling his joke three times in a row!)

Copland is Star

Star of the third quarter was All-American quarterback Aaron Copland. His selection was a suite from the opera *The Tender Land,* which Oberlin's Opera Lab played *in toto* several years ago.

After a bit of brassy Americana, we heard some rather Platonic love music—even though the strings were muted. The Party Scene may have portrayed an office Christmas party or perhaps a celebration after the Rodeo. Anyway, it is more Americana—noisy, but wholesome as all get-out!

Crowd Loved It!

The Promise of Living is first made by the English horn, properly seconded by the violas. The hymn is reaffirmed, with full brass brought into the climax. This is all just as American as Wheaties, the breakfast for champions, but to this lonesome spectator the ball seemed to remain near mid-field throughout the Copland quarter. The capacity crowd loved it—noisily.

Schumann Concludes

Following the rest period Coach Szell led his charges through Schumann's rather long *"Rhine Journey"—Symphony No. 3.* This composer's full-blown romanticisms always provide a labor of love for Coach Szell. Blocks were solid, tackles were spirited, and love of the game was much in evidence.

All the grapes on the banks of the Rhine aren't grown for nothing! In the Scherzo we hear a Rheinweinlied mixed with some dry counterpoint. The cathedral scene of the fourth movement suggests that the Rhine has now turned to eau de Cologne.

Brass Section Scores

In the last movement *gemütlichkeit* returns with charming phrases and off-beat accents. In the closing minute the brass section was sent crashing through the center of the line for the final touchdown. (This section is the Jim Brown of the Cleveland Orchestra).

Clapping hands and stamping feet brought Coach Szell back for repeated bows and sweet glances at his team after the final whistle had blown. The outcome of the game was never in doubt; the only question was how large a score Cleveland would pile up.

Impressive Exhibition

It was an impressive exhibition—a clean, hard-fought game, with no personal fouls and only rare off-side penalties. The Coach and his forces showed mid-season form, although they have not been in training camp long.

Special credit goes to the line; it was generally well sustained. There was some neat broken-field running by scatback soloists in all sections. As usual, power, speed, precision, deception and change of pace were apparent in the work of this team. We look forward to the next time they will play here. Paul Brown is not the only perfectionist coach in Cleveland!

Chapter XI

Three Rehearsal Techniques in Preparing an Orchestral Work

Plenty of orchestral players become conductors, but what conductors have become players? To quote from the old Steve Allen show, "*Why not?*" The motto of conductors for orchestral players all too often is "Theirs not to reason why; theirs but to do or die!" (A prominent European conductor called his players "stand-whores.")

Learning a new orchestral part is usually like having a role in a play without knowing what the other lines are or what the play is all about:

> (BEATRICE: . . . .)
> BENEDICK: God keep your ladyship still in that mind! so some gentleman or other shall 'scape a predestinate scratched face.
> (BEATRICE: . . . .)
> BENEDICK: Well, you are a rare *parrot-teacher.*
> (BEATRICE: . . . .)
> BENEDICK: I would my horse had the speed of your tongue, and so good a continuer. But keep your way o'God's name; I have done.

Benedick's lines *alone* certainly add up to *Much Ado About Nothing.* Isn't this like playing a single orchestral part, with no knowledge of what else goes on?

Technique I. The conductor should try to give *all* players some *knowledge of what the score is.* This makes for more intelligent, efficient, and meaningful performance. Small scores are most helpful; when they are not available, the conductor can show his large score at times to explain a point, instead of merely giving out dictatorial decrees. For contest numbers, four scores are required; the three extra copies may be useful for certain other people in addition to the judges!

The *full* score is the only satisfactory kind. When no score is available, both conductor and players are groping in the dark—not a very satisfying process. One of the most valuable aids is the small sample score now being issued by many publishers. A few of these sample scores scattered throughout the orchestra can work wonders. (Remember, in most choral music a singer can *see* what is happening in parts other than his own.)

Let's not keep the score a deep secret known *only* by the conductor! Let the players discover—hear and see—that a movement is a canon, fugue, a three-part form, or a "second rondo," in the Aeolian mode, with contrast between tutti and solo parts, etc. Such discoveries and explanations take time, but they get players *inside the music!*

Technique II.　　The conductor should have his players compare and make decisions. Which bowing or part of the bow is best for a passage? What should the phrasing be? If the balance is off, should there be more solo or less accompaniment? What accompaniment style is best for showing off a particular melody? (This is like selecting the most appropriate setting for a precious stone.) When a section is muddy, just how much spacing of the notes will best clear it up? Has the composer miscalculated? (Being human, he may have.) What should be done better to realize his intentions? Which conducting technique does the orchestra prefer for a tricky start or for resuming after a fermata?

Constantly ask the players: "Why? Why is this out of tune?" Not "You're flat!" "What is the loudest (or softest) place in the piece? Main climax? Why? *What gives contrast, variety, unity?*" Make the orchestra stop, look, listen, then decide. In this way players learn *principles applicable to all music and performances,* instead of being spoonfed "educational pablum" by the conductor.

Real Music Appreciation Added

Technique III.　　The conductor should combine performance and appreciation in rehearsals. The skillful conductor can take advantage of his students' discoveries to relate them to wider backgrounds that enlarge the players' genuine appreciation and knowledge of music, without interfering in the least with learning to play the composition being studied.

The student who really knows what a fugue is will not need to be told to bring out the subject when it appears in his orchestral part. Knowing that a selection being rehearsed is in 5-part A-B-A-C-A form, the common name for this form, its contrasts and unity—such knowledge will not hamper a player's understanding of how to interpret the piece.

Imparting this type of knowledge need not be done by long, boring, erudite lectures—it can be done in a lively, interesting manner, not requiring much rehearsal time. The popular joke about the oboist's sole interest in whether the piece was slow or fast, loud or soft, simply points up the frustration of many orchestral players and the reason for one-way traffic, left to right, in the player-conductor changeover. The present plea is for a more *active* part for players in the rehearsal process, for allowing them to join in the popular "do-it-yourself" movement.

Summary of Rehearsal Techniques

I. Try to give *all* players as much *score-knowledge* as possible, an overall view—knowing what it's all about rather than just playing one isolated part. *Intelligence, not blind stupidity.*

II. Let players compare, make decisions, *learn for themselves and apply what they learn as much as possible.* The big question is *Why?* The final aim is to make the conductor almost unnecessary: *to make students musically mature, not spoonfed infants.*

III. *Constantly combine performance and appreciation* (knowledge and love), theory and its application, thought and action. Let's have *more action based on thought and knowledge, and less blind following of conductorial decrees to do or die!* Then we'll come nearer to the ideal of treating each member of our organizations as an intelligent, worthwhile individual *now*, and perhaps as a potential conductor for the future.

In the 1970 "World of Strings," William Moennig, Jr., wrote, following a discussion with Rafael Druian advocating more concerts using symphony players in small ensembles or chamber orchestras, playing frequently all over the city:

> This would also give the player an increased sense of importance and make him a better musician by giving him more opportunity to be heard and be an individual instead of one of a hundred. Greater recognition would be given to each musician, which he does not usually receive, plus a feeling of self-respect. Many fine players now turn their backs on symphony positions and seek their feeling of self-respect in quartets in residency and teaching positions in our many fine music schools.

The above article, minus the final parenthetical section, appeared in the *Music Journal for* March, 1960, and was based on a workshop the writer conducted with the Boone, Iowa, High School Orchestra. Several later clinics suggest a continuation of the same line of thought.

Trained Seal Act?

Many highly trained and skilled musical performances are given of *we know not what*. The music has obviously been worked from the outside in, not getting in very far. The performers sometimes have as little understanding of what they have been trained to do as the seals who are taught to blow horns in a certain order, and are then thrown a fish as a reward.

If this judgment seems unduly harsh, consider two examples. 1). A good high school orchestra had just played a concert performance of Beethoven's *Egmont Overture*. The writer asked *what* they had played—what did the title mean, what was the music all about? Finally the concertmistress timidly raised her hand and said she "thought it was a play." This was the extent of the orchestra's knowledge. 2). An orchestra performed selections from *Camelot*. Questioning revealed that one girl back in the first violin section knew the story, what tunes were included in the selections played, who sang them, how they fitted in, what the words were, etc. No one else had the faintest idea about what the orchestra had played in public.

This is not to suggest that knowing all about Egmont and Camelot will substitute for learning to play the notes, of course, but some knowledge will make the performance more meaningful and enjoyable for the players, and probably for listeners, also. Orchestral players do not need to be musicologists, but if they are taught to learn their music from the inside out, they can never be accused of participating in a "trained seal act."

I recently heard a public performance of Brahms' *First Symphony* by a conservatory orchestra. My impression was that the players had "gone through the motions" of playing this work. Technique, intonation, etc., were good, but the players and conductor didn't sound as though they *meant it!* There is no thrill in hearing such performances.

A long-time symphony player recently said, in reference to his having no voice in musical affairs under proposed government subsidy of the arts: "I've *never* had any. So there's no difference!"

Knowing little or nothing about what is being performed may be par for the course. But *it adds much fuel to the current criticism of performance as an activity for its own sake!* Let the orchestra conductor examine closely his rehearsal techniques and procedures.

Interlude II: Musical Europe Tour

The New York Orchestra, Gay Gardeners, Cocktail Combo, Sidewalk Strollers, Bierkeller Kids, Palm Court Ensemble, Moonlight Serenaders, Atlantic Rollers, Happy Wanderers, Sea Ramblers, Rock Rollers, All Stars, Happy Fellas, Musical Grasshoppers, Masquerade Melodeers, Cyclopean Syncopators, Rocking Four, Atlantic Persuaders, Neptune Quartet, Late Alligators, and the Basin Quartet all provided us with music from New York to Southampton and from Le Havre back to New York. These different names applied to the same small band of musicians aboard the T.S.S. *New York*. T.S.S. stands for Twin-Screw Steamer, but Emil, our dining steward, told us confidentially that the real meaning was "Terrible Slow Ship."

Ours was the third version of a Musical Europe Tour arranged by the House of Travel of New York with Oberlin tour leaders. On the first tour in 1956 the leaders were Conservatory Director and Mrs. David Robertson. In 1957 Assistant Director and Mrs. Paul Steg were tour leaders. The summer of 1958 found my wife and me with a party of fifteen making a "Cook's Tour of Europe"—hearing music, absorbing "culture," inspecting plumbing (many substandard ratings given!), and generally promoting international good will.

On shipboard, in addition to the musical treats listed in paragraph one, we enjoyed good food, not-so-good movies, Ping Pong and other mild exercise, and many lazy hours in deck chairs. We devoured the ship's "newspaper," appropriately named *T.S.S. New York Times*, and the *Daily New Yorker*, a program of events. We read such practical information as "There are two sides to a ship, leeward and windward. Windward is the side where you put your deck chair."

In London we spent a most enjoyable evening at the Royal Festival Hall, a superb auditorium offering a beautiful view from its two dining levels overlooking the Thames. London's Festival Ballet with the London Philharmonic Orchestra presented *Les Sylphides* (Chopin) and *Graduation Ball* (Johann Strauss) with a very effective contemporary work, *The Witch Boy* (Leonard Salzedo), sandwiched between.

In marked contrast to the modern Festival Hall, Covent Garden is now more than a century old. We heard the 335th performance of *Carmen* given in this beautiful old Royal Opera House. Regina Resnik sang the title role. From a box in the golden tier overlooking the orchestra pit we noted that the young conductor, John Matheson, did a competent job with no score before him.

After the customary sightseeing of London Town, during which we took beautiful color slides of the southern exposure of the Horse Guard headed north (see photograph), we reluctantly left the city. As we drove through Banbury one of our members recited the appropriate Mother Goose rhyme. A short visit to Warwick Castle and lunch at the Porridge Pot in Warwick came next on our trip to Stratford upon Avon.

We paid our respects to the Immortal Bard and his lady friend, then went to a performance of *Pericles* at the Shakespeare Memorial Theatre. When I later told my beloved English Literature professor, Mrs. Lampson, which play we saw, she made a face like that produced by drinking very strong persimmon wine. Ignorant at the time, however, I enjoyed the play. The storm at sea was enough to give a hardened traveler *mal de mer* and the brothel scene was wholesomely bawdy. Given the chance, I would go again to see *Pericles* (without telling my friend Mrs. L.).

One of the most interesting lodging places on the entire trip was the Ettington Park Hotel, a picturesque tenth-century castle in the country, five or six miles out of Stratford. We enjoyed an after-dinner stroll in idyllic surroundings and marveled at the resplendent full dress of the headwaiter at breakfast.

After zipping through Oxford (our courier had left her bag

at Stratford; preoccupation with her loss permitted no fooling around in an old university town) and crossing a rough English Channel, we found our "permanent" bus and driver waiting at Ostend. We arrived in Brussels at eleven thirty P.M., to see a crowded, highly illuminated, beautiful city.

The Brussels World Fair needs no further publicity or description at this late date. The gypsy orchestra in the restaurant of the Hungarian Pavilion intrigued me. Their slides to imitate whistling in the march from *The Bridge on the River Kwai* made Bartók's glissandi seem halfhearted. I began to realize that the favorite selection on our tour was to be this march, performed with various nationalistic idiosyncrasies and often accompanied by the placing of a small American flag on our table. Language barriers sometimes prevented our asking how much a local group demanded *not* to play it.

In Brussels I also discovered that one of the chief duties of a tour leader is to demonstrate his vocabulary in "bawling out" any member who delays the party. This is something of an art, especially when it involves a sweet lady old enough to be one's mother. I recalled that Louis Lord, a veteran tour leader, was reputed to have raised a classic question: "Madam, are you leaving the tour before or after lunch?"

My wife (Stella A.), after much kidding about the name, finally sampled "Stella Artois," a beverage advertised all over Brussels. For fifty francs I bought a replica of the famous Mannikin Fountain. These transactions concluded our business in Brussels.

No sooner had we crossed no-man's-land into Germany than we encountered Wiener schnitzel—for lunch in the Bahnhof in Aachen and for dinner in our hotel in Cologne. (What would Europe be without Wiener schnitzel? Unimaginable! We decided the reason we saw few calves was that most of them had been slaughtered to provide tourists with a steady diet of Wiener schnitzel.) Nevertheless, it was pleasant to admire the Cologne Cathedral and to look out over the Rhine from our hotel room.

Visiting Beethoven's birthplace in Bonn was a thrill—seeing his string instruments, manuscripts of the C major quartet and

Pastoral Symphony, his ear trumpets, the death mask, and other interesting items. Beethoven's scratched-out, rewritten notes contrasted sharply with the neat, engraved-appearing manuscripts of Wagner we were soon to examine. It seemed as though Beethoven could make mistakes and correct them but Wagner could not.

Near the end of a most delightful Rhine Journey from Coblenz, I announced over the loudspeakers "Cook's Cookies leave boat at Rüdesheim." We did—*all* of us, carefully counted. A basic requirement for any tour leader is to be able to count at least as far as the number in his party. This ability will be used many times daily during the tour. In fact, one leader we met said he had reached the point in his tour where he didn't care *who* they were, just so there were fourteen of them!

After admiring the striking fortress of Würzburg and the old city walls of Nuremberg we arrived at Bayreuth. *Die Meistersinger* and *Parsifal* in the Wagner Festspielhaus were unforgettable experiences. The orchestra was superb. (Why should it be hidden, when the center of interest is so often in the pit rather than on stage?) The first violin section was composed of concertmasters from various German symphony orchestras!

The chorus was excellent; of the leading singers one of the most outstanding was the American Jerome Hines. My strongest impression of the Bayreuth performances, however, was that of an *audience* which made not a sound—no late entrances or early exits, hacking coughs, startling flashbulbs, or other distractions. Dinner during one of the hour-long intervals between acts, in a dressy, cosmopolitan crowd, was also an interesting feature.

Parsifal reminds me of Mark Twain's comment that "Wagner's terminal facilities were limited." We were flattered at the attention our box was receiving until we discovered the reason at the first interval: the Begum of Aga Khan III, a striking, gracious lady with a huge white fur neckpiece, was seated in our box with a companion. She spoke no English, but I found I could communicate in French, and have "O H. Agakhan" written on my program to prove it.

The following night we descended from the Holy Grail of

Parsifal to the big beer stein of Munich's Hofbräuhaus. Here we heard a German band present its version of *The Bridge on the River Kwai* march in the company of a former student, Dick Fiske, and other American soldiers. The next day's itinerary included a ride on the boat *Siegfried* to visit Schloss Herrenchiemsee, a magnificent palace built by Ludwig II of Bavaria. Crossing the Austrian border, we soon found ourselves in a small city of particular interest for Oberlinians at that time—Salzburg.

Mozart's hometown is a fascinating place for musicians, and hearing his music where he wrote much of it is a pleasure. Aside from its many associations with Mozart, however, this picturesque city has much to offer its visitors. We attended *Jedermann* on the Dom Platz until the performance was rained out. (A native told us it rains four hundred days a year in Salzburg, but such precipitation is nothing new to those who know that "Old Oberlin, brave Mother, Thou reignest alone.") Beautiful Mirabell Garden, Hohensalzburg, and many other attractions were visited by our group.

Mozart's tiny child's violin and bow, his concert violin (Jacobus Stainer), manuscripts and other mementos were admired in the Geburtshaus and Museum. At the Mozarteum I visited the Director, Dr. Preussner, and Professor Mueller, one of the violin teachers. In the white and gold concert hall of this famous music school we heard a fine program given by I Musici, an excellent Italian string ensemble. As we left Salzburg we felt considerable envy for the Oberlin Conservatory Juniors who were to spend a full year studying in this charming place.

The first glimpse of the beautiful blue Danube showed it to be, temporarily at least, rather a dirty brown, but pretty just the same. Vienna seemed a bit drab and somber in August; the Viennese complained that their best musicians were elsewhere at that time. One sensed some hostility to Americans here. Our local guide said: "We are musical people. Why bomb our Opera and St. Stephen's Church? What have they to do with war?" (He had not seen London.)

Some lasting memories of Vienna are these: the view of the twinkling city lights from Cobenzl high in the Vienna Woods, new wine not entirely worth the trouble of displaying green branches, the wonderful rebuilt Opera House, the painting at Schönbrunn showing Leopold and little Wolfgang Mozart in the audience at a concert following a royal wedding, the Academy of Music which set me to thinking of the incomparable Fritz Kreisler and his *Caprice Viennois,* the many statues and memorials for the great musicians who lived in Vienna. Yes, Alt Wien *was* a musical city! A concert by the Wiener Symphonie in the wonderful outdoor setting of the Arkadenhof des Neuen Wiener Rathauses on a night complete with full moon, and a performance of *Die Fledermaus* in the Redoutensaal of the Hofburg were affairs to remember.

A happy day's drive took us over the Semmering Pass and through Klagenfurt to Pörtschach on the Wörthersee. (This little resort on the "Austrian Riviera" was the summer home for Brahms while he wrote his second symphony.) A bracing swim after the hot day, an excellent dinner at the new Hotel Werzer Astoria, moonlight shining on the beautiful lake and outlining the Karawanken Alps, Japanese lanterns and gay dancing at the waterfront, all conspired to make at least one American tourist feel this to be one of the loveliest spots he had ever experienced.

The next day brought sudden contrast! We had just crossed the Italian border when our bus broke down. After laborious transfer by a single taxi to Tarvisio we took a jam-packed train to Venice, to find the sirocco blowing and the temperature standing at 104 degrees.

In the home of the Gabrieli, Vivaldi, Marcello and others we heard a very good all-Brahms concert by the Orchestra del Teatro la Fenice in the courtyard of the Ducal Palace. Afterward, we enjoyed a cooling *limonata* on St. Mark's Square, with many orchestras playing and the moon slowly measuring the Campanile—then back to the hotel to swelter all night long. No air conditioning there!

Sunday morning in St. Mark's Cathedral brought the sound of deep, rich male voices and a priest intoning the Mass. Then we took a speedboat ride to Murano Island where we admired a master glassblower at work and purchased some of his finished products. In the evening we set out in black gondolas for the colorful Gondoliers' Serenade. (It is easy to find one's way on the Grand Canal, but some of the small, unmarked side canals are more of a problem. On one of these I noted the sign "Alimentari"; this Alimentary Canal became a landmark for me.)

Our train from Venice to Florence became terribly crowded; plowing through ten cars to the diner was a major feat. Returning to our compartments one lady developed such momentum by her head-down, fullback-like rushing tactics that she overshot the goal line by two full cars!

Beautiful Florence of the Ponte Vecchio, the gleaming pink marble and golden doors, Michelangelo's *David* and other impressive sculptures, paintings galore, leatherwork, Dante's home, Rossini's tomb—it was easy to understand Albert Spalding's love for this old city where he lived as a boy. Illuminated manuscripts and leather goods were among our purchases in Florence. An evening concert in the courtyard of the Pitti Palace presented a *violinista e pianista* in a program by composers from Tuscany.

Some knowledge of music terminology pays off in Italy: "Non troppo" to a barber cutting my hair in Florence, for example. While it was hardly necessary advice in my case, I remembered that a German barber on our ship had determined to shave my head; this was carrying matters too far, definitely *troppo*.

A short stop at Arezzo gave time to photograph the statue of the celebrated monk Guido d'Arezzo, to sing "do-re-mi" in his honor, and to think of Professor Karl W. Gehrkens, who had first introduced me to Guido and his works. After lunch in Perugia, the university town high on a hill with a beautiful panorama, we drove on to visit the Church and Convent of St. Francis of Assisi and to hear his simple but moving prayer and benediction recited at his tomb.

Our first evening in Rome was spent at an outdoor concert by the Santa Cecilia Orchestra in the Stadio di Domiziano. This excellent orchestra boasts a string section with beautiful, full sound and fine precision. (Italy was the birthplace of our modern string instruments; one of my violins was made by Francesco de Emiliani in Rome in 1727.)

Sightseeing makes clear the reason Respighi was moved to compose his *Fountains of Rome* and *Pines of Rome*. We were much impressed by St. Peter's (and its carefully inlaid floor-markers showing how much longer it is than assorted other cathedrals), but the terrific mob in the Vatican Museum took some of the pleasure out of viewing its treasures. After seeing, during the day in Rome, the real settings for the three acts of *Tosca* it was pleasant at night to attend a performance of the opera (part of the Puccini Centenary Celebration) at the picturesque Terme di Caracalla. The singers (including Tagliavini) and orchestra were quite good, but this huge outdoor "bathroom" is almost too large for "singing in," at least in public.

Excellent food at Romolo's in Rome, the Albergo Miramare in Formia, and the Hotel Carlton in Sorrento deserves mention. The men in our party conducted customary research in the ruins of Pompeii. A day spent on Capri, with visits to the Blue Grotto, Anacapri, and San Michele, sampling octopus, fried eel, and other delicacies, and closing with an evening carriage ride up the hillside from Sorrento with "Bella Stella" was one of the most memorable of the tour.

An alumnus of M.I.T. in our party did not agree with my suggestion that the Leaning Tower of Pisa might have been designed by an engineer from his alma mater. We did agree on enjoying our guide's singing of chords in the marble Baptistry, where they reverberated sonorously. After the scenic Bracco Pass and Italian Riviera (Rapallo, Santa Margherita, and Portofino) we continued to Genoa, home of Columbus and Paganini. Here we found the former much better known and honored than the latter, whose explorations were limited to four short strings and whose discoveries were in violin technique.

While Pisa had its flower calendar showing the day, month, and date by flowers planted every day, Genoa had Columbus' three ships portrayed in flowers on a hillside. How much pleasure flowers, gardens, and parks provided on our trip! Europeans certainly love them.

One Italian philosopher seemed to sum up a prevalent opinion about us Americans: "Some day you die. What's your big hurry?" (This impressed me, as I had already found the tour so strenuous that I seemed to have lost nearly 100 pounds; I weighed 170 in New York and only 77 in Rome!)

In Milan, which boasts one of the finest cathedrals to be found anywhere, is La Scala—not a large opera house, but what traditions! A striking bust of Toscanini, mementos of Caruso, Giuseppe Verdi (called "Joe Green" by one gentleman in our party), and other musical greats are found in La Scala's museum. In a Milan church our courier showed us a small canvas as the original of *The Last Supper* by da Vinci. This did not pass inspection by our experienced art critics; they led us to the refectory of the church where we saw the large "restored original" fresco.

Stresa, on Lago Maggiore, provided a scenic overnight stop. Toscanini had maintained a summer home on a small island in this peaceful lake. Lunch on the col of the Simplon Pass in Switzerland gave time to admire one of the trip's most breathtaking panoramas. A visit to the Castle of Chillon and the drive around pretty Lac Leman to Lausanne completed another satisfactory day. Shopping for watches in Bern, lunching at the Kornhaus Keller, visiting Basel, driving on to Mulhouse—another day swiftly disappeared.

An unfortunate breakfast experience in the Gare at Belfort, France, did little toward improving international relations, and I am afraid we Ugly Americans were to blame. After a long day's drive through Dijon and Fontainebleau, where we visited the famous Music School for Americans, we arrived in Paris to find that our ship was delayed and would not sail until August 23. We were to enjoy a full week in Paris!

We attended a Mass in La Madeleine, where Saint-Saëns was for twenty years the organist. In the gardens of Versailles the Spectacle of Light and Sound, with music by Jacques Ibert, dramatically filled one of our evenings. At L'Opéra-Comique we were most delightfully surprised by an opera none of us had heard in the States—Gounod's light and tuneful *Mireille*. In the same intimate opera house we enjoyed an evening of ballet: *Blue Danube* (Strauss), *Archaic Suite* (Honegger), *L'Amour*

Sorcier (Falla), and *Frères Humains* (Rhapsody in Blue—Gershwin).

We did the usual sightseeing in Paris, including the Folies Bergère. Ah, *quel folie!* This show had not changed much in four years; the star was the same, Yvonne Menard. A pleasant evening was spent exploring Montmartre in the moonlight—Sacré Coeur, Place du Tertre, enticing narrow side streets—until the chilly night air began to make me think of the ending of *La Bohème.* Of course, the women in the party shopped in the well-known Parisian stores and visited Christian Dior's and similar establishments. (Rumor had it that one of our ladies took fifty dresses with her and bought more abroad!)

Travel agencies well know how long tourists require to become satiated. By the end of our week in Paris, a frequent comment was "I don't want to see anything more." One gentleman allowed he would be glad to get back to a country where he would know what was going on. So it was not *too* reluctantly that we departed for the buoys and gulls of Le Havre.

Breakfast on shipboard once more was a treat after the continental jaw- and tooth-breakers. North Atlantic gales plus Hurricane Daisy kept a few of our party feeling queasy on the way home. Holding on to a rail during a shipboard church service, I felt that one portion of the benediction—"Keep us from falling"—was never more appropriate! But, isn't the full moon beautiful on the water? And isn't it fun to watch the college students' romances (and some older people's too) blooming all over the ship's decks? Isn't it exciting to catch the first glimpse of Long Island? Then, at the very end of an eight-week trip, isn't it a pleasure to see home and family again?

How many times, during the winter months, color slides and *Holiday's* articles and pictures recall places you visited and the many thrills you experienced! How nice at Christmas to hear from friends, old and new, who were on the tour with you! How quickly disagreeable incidents disappear among the hosts of happy memories! And how soon you begin to have furtive little ideas—most attractive, really—which clearly prove you're beginning to plan for *another* European tour!

dare say that is still true!" This beautiful school, rebuilt since the war, has names and atmosphere. Much time could be spent here, as well as at La Scala and the Cathedral. Near La Scala Opera House was Ristorante Concerto, with a smaller room appropriately named Concertino. Via Dogana in Milano reminded me that in European cities it was difficult to decide whether to see the sights or watch the sidewalk for dogpiles.

In the Teatro Nuovo we heard an all-Mendelssohn program played by the Orchestra Sinfonica Stabile da Camera, with violinist Isidor Lateiner as soloist. There was more of the crisp, darting bowing, and how these Italian strings *sing!* Some Mendelssohn they sang like Puccini, but what a pleasure to hear beautiful, expressive tone.

At Ricordi's, some Pergolesi string music, edited by Renato Fasano as part of the Collegium Musicum Italicum Series, was purchased. We then departed for the Riviera, thinking of the Italian maid who knocked on our hotel door and asked "Sonata? Campanella?" How musical can you get?

Driving up the Rhone Valley reminded me of friend David Mattern's joke: *Pas de lieu Rhône que nous.* We sang *Sur le Pont d' Avignon* at the appropriate spot, then went on to Moulins, where a woman in the music store said the strings were way down in France—The Old Refrain. I noted a sign by a bridge over the Allier River, "Défense d'uriner." They wanted no pollution there, even in 1962!

We attended a musical service in the thirteenth-century Cathédrale St.-Étienne de *Bourges*, with its unique five portals The priest gave one of the best talks on music I've ever heard. Here is a sample of his thinking: Sculpture and painting are damaged by time (the figures at the entrance to the Cathedral were disfigured at the time of the French Revolution), but a Schubert melody remains intact through time.

Visits to various chateaux and Chartre's cathedral were made on the way to Paris, where we arrived December 4, to receive the good news that our grandson, Jeffrey, had arrived back in Ohio!

In Paris we had an eight-day musical orgy, including two

days with three concerts each. The Chamber Orchestra of Hamburg, with Friedrich Wührer as violinist and leader, gave a good concert in the Salle Gaveau. After innumerable hearings of the Bach *Double Concerto in D minor,* one is tempted to ask: Has there ever been a performance with both the solo violin parts (especially the second violin) exactly in tune?

École Normale de Musique de Paris was old, but had impressive names for its rooms: Casals, Honegger, Thibaud, etc. Alfred Cortot, president and cofounder, had died the past summer. There were tears in the eyes of his secretary as she showed his still green plants in the office. She reported many youths studying violin and cello there, but few viola and almost no bass students. There were fewer strings than before. She asked if our marching bands were amusement or music? This was a school founded upon the realization that most musical careers are destined to include teaching.

In the little old hall of the École we heard the Orchestra de Chambre Pasdeloup under Merle Portalès. Gérard Poulet was violin soloist in the Bach *Concerto in E major*—about the sixth time we had heard this work on the trip. The string players in this group, mostly women, all had relaxed fingers, very fast vibrato, and free, incisive bowing.

The Conservatoire National Supérieur de Musique was older and "dingier" than before, but still producing the goods, as shown by its list of prizewinners in recent international competitions and the sounds coming from the rooms. Limits were placed on the number of "femmes" to be admitted in many categories—they cannot exceed *la moitié*—a good idea. What a school!

Salle Pleyel was the setting for a concert by the Orchestre des Concerts Colonne, conducted by "le jeune et prestigieux Robert Bronstein." Once more we had a young conductor much concerned with his motions and appearance—the willowy left hand, the imitation of Karajan. The young man knew his scores and was musical, but in this program of music by the three B's, there was entirely too much of a fourth B.

A very old hall, almost round, with fine acoustics was the

Théatre des Champs-Élysées, where at ten in the morning we heard an interesting Répétition Générale Publique of the Société des Concerts du Conservatoire, under Jean Gitton. Idyl Biret was the exciting soloist in the Tchaikovsky *Piano Concerto,* and *Psalm 47* by Florent Schmitt proved to be a big, thrilling, effective work for soprano, chorus, and orchestra. This was a good orchestra, despite a few rehearsal boo-boos which mattered little.

In the afternoon we heard Le Trinome (Le Trio à Clavier de Paris) play a very refined concert in the Comédie des Champs-Élysées. That evening we were in the Théatre National de l' Opéra (almost one hundred years old), where the golden bosomy dames protected us from above during performances of a ballet, *Suite en Blanc* to music by Lalo, and the one hundredth production here of *Jeanne au Bûcher,* Claudel's poem and Honegger's music, conducted by Louis Fourestier. *Joan at the Stake* was colorful and different. The red flames and breaking of her chains at the end made a strong climax.

At the Salle Gaveau two concerts by the Quatuor Parrenin presented the complete six quartets by Bartók. This was a top-notch French quartet, excelling in ponticello and tasto scherzo-type passages and in pizzicati, with a big variety of sounds and colors. It was interesting to note Bartók's progress through his six works. Since the last quartet is mature, not so wild or concerned with "effects," and closes with an introspective slow movement, it was wise not to end the series with this. The Fifth Quartet, most striking of all, was excellent to end the cycle. The great majority of the enthusiastic, "bravoing," unison-clapping audience were college age.

What other city offers five major symphony concerts at the same hour? (Sunday, 17:45 h.) (We were soon to discover that Tokyo had seven symphony orchestras!) We selected Concerts Lamoreux at Salle Pleyel, conducted by Bernard Haitink of Amsterdam. This was a fine orchestra (the two harpists were the only women) and Haitink's performance of the Brahms *Fourth Symphony* was one of the best I've heard—thrilling and beautiful.

In the Salle des Conservatoires a concert was given by the

Orchestre Philharmonique de la R.T.F. (French Radio-Tele-
vision), with Bulgarian Constantin Iliev conducting. Most stands
in the string section were chaired (shared?) by one man, one
woman. Two works on the program by Bulgarian composers produced the wildest, most "unbuttoned" playing heard on our
trip. Honegger's *Symphonie No. 3,* following a hearing of his
Jeanne the previous night at the Opéra, made us think he seemed
to be for the French what Bruckner was for the Austrians. Honegger stressed the "religious character of my music"; we noted
quite a combination of elements in his music.

A visit to the office of *Les Jeunesses Musicales de France* led
to interesting discussion and some of their publications. Nineteen countries had this "Musical Youth" organization, each with
its separate organization, but they came together for a meeting
every year. We had noted the work of this organization in various
countries. It appeared to be a very interesting and valuable
movement.

Back in New York again, we had our first chance to hear a
concert in the newly completed Philharmonic Hall, to admire
some of its features, and to find that from where we sat there
was a lack of bass sound, with the range from violin open E
up almost too brilliant. Balance seemed to be the acoustical
problem.

The New York Philharmonic Orchestra, with Lorin Maazel
conducting and Christian Ferras violin soloist, played two *Fifth
Symphonies* (Mendelssohn and Beethoven) with the Berg *Violin
Concerto* sandwiched between. There were no women in this
orchestra, but it seemed to have become second class, with nothing really outstanding about it. Berg, in the French treatment of
Ferras, was the feature of this concert, played with fine tone
and technic. Maazel impressed us as having a long way to go at
that time before he would be a first-class conductor. Rather
awkward and "jumpy," he overconducted, but the orchestra kept
itself clean and did not get much involved in the music.

Camelot at the Majestic Theater was a very good show.
Americans really feel the beat of such music. "A Vivaldi Evening"
with the Festival Orchestra conducted by Thomas Dunn filled

Philharmonic Hall twice in one evening and was a treat to hear. The finale was the *Four Seasons,* with Gerald Tarack violin soloist in Spring and Autumn, Isidore Cohen in Summer and Winter. What a composer was the Red Priest of Venice!

The Juilliard School of Music listed sixty-six violinists and plenty of cellists for two orchestras. There were only about three viola majors, the remainder of the viola sections being violinists. More bassists were needed. A rehearsal of the Juilliard Orchestra I under Jean Morel was devoted to *Feu d'artifice* by Stravinsky, *Symphony No. 7* by Piston, and the Brahms *Second Piano Concerto.* This was a good orchestra and conductor, but hard to work with; the students had technique, but one sensed that they wanted to be virtuosi rather than orchestra players.

A short visit to the High School of Performing Arts completed the "educational" part of our trip, followed by a Town Hall recital by the Marlboro Trio. The ensemble played very well, but a gentleman across the aisle mistook Brahms' *Trio* for his *Lullaby!* The first performance of David Amram's *Dirge and Variations* reminded me that this young man had once played horn in my Training Orchestra and was reputed to have said, "Oberlin is a place where they teach kids to hate music." Well, you can't win them all, as Denny McLain once said. We enjoyed the reverence shown by the violinist in his "let us pray" posture while the pianist or cellist played.

After expressing our reverence for the Christmas season by attending the *Nutcracker Ballet* at City Center and the Christmas Show at Radio City Music Hall, we departed for home, softly mumbling, "It is enough!" (By February we had recovered sufficiently to start out on a four-month Cooks' Tour to Japan. But that is another story, about which I have already written much.)

Chapter XIX

The Chicken or The Egg?

Ivan Galamian and many others emphasize the importance of the mind as the central control in music-making. "Conception, then realization." Technique is the carrying out by the body of commands emanating from the mind. Casals says, "Everything from the heart." Whether we use "mind" or "heart" as the keyword, there is a *center from* which actions emanate. This is the *"inside-out" theory of operation* in making music. (Mind and heart are two different centers, however.)

F. Matthias Alexander of London, whose theory of the all-important *primary control of the self* has been very influential, emphasizes the relation of head to neck to body. When this is balanced and natural, the "command currents" flow freely and are not impeded. The many music teachers who stress movement as originating in the large muscles of the back are continuing the process from a center out to the fingertips. "Use the body as a whole." (The idea of concentrating on the base joints of the fingers of the left hand moves the focus out toward the fingertips, but still centers attention back of the fingers themselves.) These theories progress always *from the whole to the parts.*

The many writings which present bone structure, muscle systems, and how they work suggest that the "feel" and knowledge of the body are the starting points in technique. When such factors are understood and operating efficiently, the body is ready, willing, and able to carry out the commands of the mind or heart. In other words, when you have technique you are able to express yourself. If you don't have technique, you can't get your message through, no matter how strongly it may be felt. This theory operates from the *outside in.* "Concentrate on the fingertips" is advice sometimes given to the student violinist.

Technical control is the first thing taught by some teachers.

As in Europe, should *solfège* (command of pitch and rhythm) be learned before the study of any instrument is begun? Or, as in the Orient, is the first step to fill the *ear* with fine music and performance—*listen* now, *play* later? Or is *instrumental technique* (physical command of the instrument) the first thing to be acquired, and at a very young age? Aren't all of these things necessary, and arguments concerning them about as fruitful as debates on the title of this chapter?

At any rate, much has been written which applies to mastery of the physical part of making music. A sample of many magazine articles may include: "Conscious Direction in String Practice" by Francis Tursi (*American Music Teacher*, May-June, 1960); "Awareness, Freedom and Muscular Control" by Frank Pierce Jones (*Musical America*, Jan. 1, 1949); "The Physical Sensation Comes First" by Abby Whiteside (*Musical America*, Dec. 15, 1951); "Relax and Be Beautiful" by Gayelord Hauser (*This Week*, Oct. 9, 1960).

F. M. Alexander's books, *The Use of the Self* (Dutton, 1932) and *The Universal Constant in Living* (Dutton, 1941), have been studied by many musicians. H. M. Shapiro's book is called *The Physical Approach to Violinistic Problems* (Omega Music Edition, 1954). A book by Fred Rosenberg is titled *The Violin— The Technic of Relaxation and Power—A Study of the Internal Laws of Coordination* (Powell Publishing Co., 1961). *Senso- Motor Study and Its Application to Violin Playing* by Frederick Polnauer and Morton Marks (ASTA-Presser) appeared in 1964. Kato Havas writes in her book *A New Approach to Violin Playing* (Bosworth & Co., 1961), "Only those who are free to derive pleasure from music are in turn able to give pleasure."

Professor Paul Rolland's recent series of fifteen films (available from Theodore Presser Co., May, 1972) on "The Teaching of Action in String Playing" provides "guides for the systematic development of natural playing movements, free of excessive tension. The feel of correct motion patterns and use of the body as a whole are taught through the Action Studies, which are exercises in movement and rhythm."

Group Encounter Therapy, or the "Esalen Approach," has led to a flood of discussion and writing. A book, *Sense Relaxation* (Below your mind) by Bernard Gunther (Macmillan Co., 1968), advises us to "get out of your minds and back into your bodies." (This sounds curiously like advice from Shinichi Suzuki!) More sensitive physical sensations and group relations are sought today by many means in music teaching and study.

The Phsysiology of Violin Playing by Otto Szende and Mihaly Nemessuri (Collet's Publishers, available Theodore Presser, 1971) should be mentioned as a recent book in the ASTA list. One lifetime is much too short to make a thorough study of all the factors discussed in the present chapter.

The writer enjoys both chicken and egg. They are equally necessary and useful. What difference does it make *which* came first?

Chapter XX

The Music Man

Meredith Willson ("And There I Stood With My Piccolo") wrote a musical show, *The Music Man,* which was later made into a movie. Since Mr. Willson was a native of Mason City, Iowa, the movie version of the show was premiered in his hometown, which responded appropriately by hosting a contest for marching bands. (Never mind the Russians' attempts to really *educate* their kids, as long as our schools devote time, energy, and money to such worthwhile things as marching bands! The Russians may boast of their Bolshoi Ballet, but we have numerous Band Ballets. We counter their Moscow Music with our Michigan Maneuver. We can even spell "Ohio" in script!)

The Willson bit of Americana features the doings of one "Professor" Harold Hill, a genuine "con man," a traveling salesman who sells, then travels immediately. The Professor invades an innocent Iowa village and by his fast talk succeeds in selling a gold brick in the form of band instruments and uniforms. (Just the thought of what is going to happen promptly improves the character of the kids in the town. One particularly troublesome case is solved at once—a problem child becomes an outstanding leader. Always remember: "The boy who blows a horn will never blow a safe!")

Professor Hill knows nothing at all about music. His instruction features the "think" school: "*Think* how Beethoven's *Minuet in G* goes." But just as the time comes for him to skeedaddle to find suckers in another town, the Professor discovers that this time it is *true* love, for the village librarian who stands for all that is right and teaches piano on the side. The outraged citizens prepare the tar and feathers and catch up with the music man. Things are getting tense!

But by golly, just in the nick of time, some kids show up and prove the validity of the "think" school. With no instruction at all, they play Beethoven's *Minuet in G* and spare the Professor the tar and feathers. This miracle accomplished, the final one is easy.

The pulse-pounding finale shows a large and brassy (seventy-six trombones, you know) uniformed marching band swinging down Main Street. And who is prancing around out in front of the gorgeous, barelegged majorettes? Why, Professor Harold Hill, of course. (One can easily see the tassels of the pure Ioway corn gently sway in the breeze.)

Shucks, folks, how can the strings ever compete with instruments that play themselves?

Chapter XXI

The General Program for
the Training of String Teachers

(Music Education Seminar: "The String Program in the Public Schools") New England Conservatory, Boston, Mass., June 29, 1964

Introduction

Since I am a midwesterner holding forth in the cultural hub of America for the first time, I decided to consult reports on two meetings held in the east within the past year. The first was a Seminar on Music Education, held at Yale University in June of 1963 and sponsored by the Federal Government. Here are a few quotes from a report of the seminar:

> Reforms in teaching science and mathematics, brought about by distinguished scientists and mathematicians working through the prestige and good offices of the Government, have caused an educational revolution from primary grades on up. Were similar reforms needed in one of the arts? The answer was emphatically *affirmative*.
> Educators feel the need for close contact with the living world of musical creation and performance, and practicing musicians are sensitive to the need for close involvement in the educational process from the lowest grades.
> In most schools, in the elementary grades, untrained classroom teachers are charged with the responsibility of giving children the basic musical skills which the teachers themselves do not possess, and the means and equipment provided for the purpose of accomplishing this hopeless goal are almost invariably inadequate and antimusical.

After reading the report, I asked myself this question: In the field of strings, should we expect people to teach what they don't know and can't do themselves? Boola, boola!

The transcript of the Tanglewood String Symposium, held last August and sponsored by the Boston Symphony Orchestra at its Berkshire Music Center, contains many interesting statements which I should enjoy discussing. Time forbids; I shall quote just one sample of the repartee as an introduction to my paper:—

> MR. STUART CANIN: So many of the public school teachers, who are teaching strings in the grade schools to beginners, are former clarinetists who have exactly sixteen weeks or one semester or something like that in learning how to teach violin, viola, and cello. I think this is an extremely difficult thing to overcome.
>
> MR. RICHARD BURGIN: Doesn't this pertain to the curriculum that we have adopted in some of the music schools called "music education"?
>
> MR. CANIN: Yes, exactly. We have waited this long to say *the dirty word!*

End of quotation. Now that the dirty word has been brought out into the open I shall get on with my subject.

Cradle to grave is the new and sensible span for the string instruments in musical education of the future. Specifically, this covers the range from the one-and-one-half-year-old Kataoka child in Japan to Pablo Casals, playing and still learning at eighty-seven—or, still more personally, the range from the white-haired oldsters in my community orchestra on down to my three-year-old granddaughter, now learning to play the violin.

The public school phase covers only one-sixth (or thereabouts) of the average lifetime today. In the educational turmoil and frantic experimentation of our time, in the universal quest for excellence, and in the crowded curricula of our schools, I believe the only areas of music study deserving serious consideration are those which offer lifelong opportunities on a rewarding scale. In instrumental music the strings are in a unique position in this regard. Judged by the same criteria, the high school marching band which functions for only a fractional part, say one-third, of each of the four high school years (comprising one-third of the public school years, whose total we have set at one-sixth of a lifetime) can hardly justify any inclusion at all in school curricula, much less the dominant position it has assumed in the music departments of many school systems today. The time is indeed ripe for the long, hard looks now being focused on music in our schools!

"Lifelong pleasure in recreating some of the world's greatest musical literature, written for the finest musical media time has evolved—this is the prospect which lies ahead for the person who learns to play a string instrument. Isn't it worth the effort of a trip which may require more time than the shortest one on record?" (Quote from the Introduction to my book, *String Teaching and Some Related Topics.*) How long is the trip (study of a string instrument to reach an adequate level to perform great music)? Ten years is a figure often given. Starting study at age ten thus seems a bit late. The period from kindergarten to tenth grade (age five to fifteen) is better, and a preschool start seems best. How about ages three to thirteen (eighth grade)? What changes would be appropriate in public school instrumental music if our first-graders were playing Seitz, Vivaldi, or Bach concertos on one-fourth-size violins? And what changes will be needed in the training of public school music *teachers* who will work with such children?

These are speculations about coming events. Now, back to earth with some recent nontheoretical experiences! (1) My observation of a well-known clinician working with a beginning string orchestra of elementary school children at a state music teachers' meeting: Sound is horrible, terribly out of tune and awful quality. But clinician pays extravagant compliments, even praising the intonation! Are we kidding anyone but *ourselves*? (2) "Musica Viva" concert of present-day compositions by Tonhalle-Orchester in Zürich, Switzerland—assistant concertmaster gets carried away, breaks top two of his metal strings at once; they can't take it! Are such music and violin-playing winning friends and influencing people *for* the strings? (3)

Guest-conducting afternoon rehearsals and evening concert of an all-city junior high orchestra, I did my best in the time available, but the grumble of the cello-bass line, wrong fingerings, and other poor playing fundamentals, the difficulty in trying to keep a large group together in a live gym—again and again I asked myself, *Why* are we giving a public performance tonight? *What* are we proving? Isn't there a limit even to mother love?

What I have been emphasizing so far is the huge gap between the theoretical justifications for assigning an important place to the strings in musical education and what actually is happening in the world of strings in far too many instances. This gap *must* be closed, and the present seminar is a very worthy attempt at closing it.

Preparation of String Teachers

In the current stampede to avoid the much-criticized "education" or "methods" courses, more and more emphasis is being placed on "performance" in teacher-training programs. We constantly hear of new "cultural centers," centers for the "performing arts," but no new centers for the "teaching arts!" The trend is to place the specific teacher-training portion of the curriculum at the end of the program. In the Royal Music Schools of England the prospective string teacher studies music *only* for three years (or until he passes the required musical standards for his diploma), then usually goes to another school for a year of teacher-training work. In our country, the Master of Arts in Teaching degree is taken in a fifth year following a four-year bachelor's curriculum that is strictly academic (or musical, as this idea is applied to our field). Today, we must first of all know our subject (that is, be musicians) before we *start* to become teachers, it seems.

I confess to resenting bitterly the cynical idea that failure in the freshman string performance examination is the prerequisite for entrance into the field of music education as a string teacher. There can be no intelligent criticism of music education in our schools if teachers are selected through rejection from another field! I have no sympathy whatsoever with "artist-teachers" who delight in making cracks about music education and then advise their failing students to go into it. Criticism of a situation one has helped to create implies either stupidity or colossal nerve!

Even more cynical is the inevitable disillusion of most of our "performance" majors, who dream of some vaguely glamorous performing career in blissful ignorance of the number of children half their age who play better than *they* ever will! But most cynical of all is the "expert" who has never taught children in a public school in his life, yet pontificates publicly that there has been no improvement in public school music in fifty years! One of the most damning statements I have ever heard was made by a musician about a teacher-trainer: "She has high ideals for other people." Leaders today should have *proven* high ideals for themselves, as well. Enough catharsis!

There is great emphasis on improving education, especially *higher education,* today. Frankly, I'm more impressed with what Mr. Suzuki is doing than by the fact that the University of X has flunked out two thousand students in one quarter. The place to start improving education of any kind is *at the beginning,* not at the top! This is certainly true of string education at present, and I consider the most important work in strings now being done in our country to be with preschool children. Likewise, the most important part of the training of string teachers is their preparation to participate in improving teaching from a very early starting age, according to the new concept.

In the teacher-training institutions good work in learning more literature and technique of the student's major string instrument will continue to be most important for a long time to come. Major string teachers should not be the kind who regard all their teaching as wasted time which they *should* be spending in practice for their next playing engagement! String quartet and other one-to-a-part ensembles should be emphasized also. The allotment of very large portions of the students' time to an orchestra which is considered primarily as a prestige-winning, concert-giving organization that attempts to outdo professional groups is a mistake for technically immature string players. Their annual jury exams and recital appearances prove that excessive time spent in orchestra harms their individual playing, and the conductors of professional orchestras for whom graduates audition corroborate this opinion. The years that provide the last chance for many students to improve themselves individually should not be sacrificed to the greater glory of an institution through its performing organizations. Status-seeking, public-relations-crazy administrators are to blame here. Their number is legion!

What about the string instruments other than a student's major? The better he knows them, the better string teacher and orchestra conductor he will be. Hopefully, his experience on them will include not only homogeneous and heterogeneous classes, but some private study also. The high school orchestra conductor should be able to finger and bow, first-hand, each of the string parts to the music he conducts. He should also be trained to conduct much better than he usually does. This is basic for the director of school music groups and takes precedence over such "breadth" courses as college math or science.

Wind and percussion instruments pose a thorny problem in the training of the string teacher. For the future, in my opinion, he should not be trained on the assumption that he is going to teach them. His training in them should be devoted to helping him deal with these instruments in the context of the orchestras he will conduct. Furthermore, it may well be that a wind major in the future will find that a semester or year of string class will not prepare him to cope technically even with the first-grade violinist who plays a Vivaldi concerto! *It appears to me more and more futile to expect wind majors to carry the ball for the strings.* If we are really serious about improving the string situation, *every* string graduate must have at least a minimum of teaching preparation. The possibilities for the future are both exciting and confusing.

The ability to play and improvise piano accompaniments, albeit simple ones, is a considerable asset to the public school string teacher. Study of functional piano is a reasonable requirement in his training curriculum.

Some experience in eurythmics is of value to the string teacher-conductor. Later I hope to show some combinations of eurythmics and string study which seem worthwhile to me.

The history of the development of our string instruments, their literatures and techniques, should be known by teachers. The life story of old instruments in use today can be presented in an interesting way, and old instruments may provide a visible link with the past of a kind not too common in our young country. The strings have their full share of history and romance, on which an astute teacher can capitalize.

May I insert here a few notes written for my own college string classes of the school year just finished?

As far as the strings are concerned, the key points now seem to me to be:

1. They must be started as early as possible, violin from three years on, cello four-five on, viola transfer from violin for those suited to the larger, deeper instrument (by lower grade school); bass transfer from cello for those suited to larger, deeper instrument (¼-size for upper grade school).

2. Tone *must* be good from the beginning.

3. Good intonation and rhythm must be clearly established from the beginning.

4. Good, natural feeling must be present in the body from the beginning—the mechanics must be right.

5. *Musical* education must be stressed from the start; the child must at all times "hear" what he is trying to produce. This ear approach must come at first through good recordings or live models. Later it may come from solfège and reading music.

6. There must be mastery from the start. What is learned must be reviewed, used, and built upon. It must "stick."

7. The teacher should urge the student to excel him, and be happy when the student does.

8. The moral phase of music study needs to be reemphasized. Many people are getting tired of "scientific debauchery" in education!

9. The stupid idea of "improving things from the top," of snobbish emphasis on "higher education" needs to be scuttled!

The place to start improving is in the beginning, preschool education. We have "let go" what is probably the most important period in life and concentrated on so-called "higher education."

My general plan for a semester string class in 1964 included:

1. By ear (live and recorded) all of Suzuki Volume I (original). Transpose to D, G, C and keys better for lower instruments. *Tone* all the way.
2. By eye, Applebaum *String Builder,* Books 1, 2, 3. Tone and
other playing fundamentals. Some learning *by eye only.*
3. Other ensemble and orchestra music as time permits.
4. Assigned reading of latest literature on strings.
5. In class, full list of questions on my book and notes from
my travel during sabbatical year; go through some material from
my new book.

Theory is of obvious importance to any string player. Interval-
knowledge and harmonic thinking provide the only intelligent
musical foundation for building string playing. And counterpoint
and simultaneous harmony are particularly essential for any
musician who produces one tone at a time. Form is basic for *any*
musician.

All this seems trite and redundant, yet our commencement
this month was marked by the absence of a number of senior
performers who did not receive their degrees because they
flunked theory (and possibly other courses, too). This failure
was not due to their inability to do the course work, but to de-
liberate cutting of classes and disregard of assignments. Such
contempt of theory in favor of additional practice time on the
major instrument is not only condoned but even encouraged by
some teachers of applied music. Perhaps some of the blame
should go to over-intellectualized and uninspired theory teachers
who fail to give their students any feeling of connection between
what goes on in theory class and practical music making. I
should also like to suggest that in the case of many string students the frantic grasping for practice time during the college
years indicates a too-late start on their instruments, and con-

sequent arrival at college age without either technical or musical foundations which should have been formed years earlier. No amount of scrambling in college will enable these students to catch up with the fortunate individuals whose foundations in music were built at optimum ages!

When I brought a gifted thirteen-year-old girl violinist to the Conservatory to play a recital, our office secretary asked, "What are you trying to do, show up our seniors?" I answered "No, but they should know such people exist and are not uncommon." The same thought came to mind when Mr. Suzuki's fourteen-year-old pupil was playing the Chausson *Poème* and our concertmistress, who was to play the piece with orchestra the following week, got up and left. (Our "leader" played it well, too, but apparently this performance by a girl eight years younger was too much for her to "stomach"!)

Academic requirements are in part set up for meeting certification demands, but I believe a course in speech may be of greater value to the string teacher-conductor than a course in college math. Likewise, a course in acting and stage deportment may have more practical value for him than some science courses. Breadth is very desirable, but competence in one's profession is even more desirable!

As suggested before, required methods and education courses, etc., are being pared to the core. Here are some examples from my own school: The course in supervision and administration is dropped as an undergraduate requirement for a music education major. Functional piano, vocal ensemble, some practical instrumentation are to be absorbed into theory and conducting. Materials course is to be absorbed into student teaching seminar and conducting. Course, General Music in the Elementary School, will no longer be required of instrumental majors. Details vary in different schools, but the trend is unmistakable.

One phase of teacher-training that should *not* be reduced is observation and participation in a variety of actual teaching situations. The resident-intern form of student teaching may not be practical for all schools, but the apprentice teacher should not be limited to one level only (say elementary school string classes) for all his student teaching experience.

The future string teacher in America will need training in and observation of good teaching of very young children. This need cannot possibly be met by a "correspondence course" or by a day or week spent in listening to some teacher tell about it. I shudder to think of the results of a lot of American teachers' enthusiastically jumping on the Suzuki bandwagon and starting many young children on small violins without the faintest idea of what the method is all about, or in the mistaken belief that there is some "magic" about it that produces miracles without work! The amount of damage to the string cause that may come from a frantic, ignorant, and halfbaked rush to emulate Suzuki without fully understanding him staggers the imagination and will last for years to come. American string teachers will do their profession a great service by not starting such a movement until they really understand how it works and have double-checked their own patience and endurance to insure following through to a successful conclusion!

To sum up in a general way the relative importance of the different areas that are included in the undergraduate training of the public school string teacher, without being dogmatic about specific courses that must be required in each area, the following percentages for credits and time seem reasonable to me:

50 percent Applied Studies = 62-68 semester hours (major instrument, other string instruments, piano, winds and percussion; small and large ensemble, conducting)

20 percent Music Theory and History = 25-27 hours (includes practical instrumentation, eurythmics, course in baroque period, in addition to usual courses)

20 percent Liberal Arts = 25-27 hours (English, speech, psychology and education, elective choice)

10 percent Music Education = 13-14 hours (observation and student teaching, courses in instrumental music in preschool period, elementary and secondary schools)

The total hours, ranging from 125 to 136, lead to a Bachelor of Music degree, the same as given to a straight performance major. If such a division of subjects and credit hours does not lead to full teacher certification in some states, it should gain a provisional certificate at least; the remaining requirements can be met later. The first and most important aim of undergraduate curricula is to produce competency in a field, not to meet every state's requirements for certification. First things first, then other matters may be dealt with.

Chapter XXII

Mother Nature's Applause

(Chapel Talk, 1965)

Books on music history and appreciation in my student days usually contained a statement to the effect that music is the handmaiden of religion. I do not know what today's histories have to say on this subject, and "appreciation" is not a word in good standing now. We have plenty of music to eat by, to study by, to sleep by, and so on. And, praise be, we still have some music *to listen by.*

Anyone who has sung in the Oberlin Musical Union, the Chapel Choir, or the College Choir is well aware of the connection between music and religion. In fact, the repertoire of M.U. through the years suggests that the connection is rather on the macabre side. We must remember, however, that there have always been some pretty good composers who were "naïve" enough to experience emotions after the death of a loved one.

For some people the connection between music and religion extends even beyond *the word.* For them, musical tone may have the power to carry on where the word leaves off.

To return to vocal music, I believe St. Benedict was said to have advocated corporal punishment for those who sang out of tune. If "capital" were substituted for "corporal," St. Benedict might have solved the overpopulation problem in the world today. He would have made slight inroad into the Oberlin choral groups under their skilled conductors. The long-continued success of the Oberlin College Choir is due in part, of course, to the fine ear and musicianship of its director. His "built-in metronome" (or "thing-a-ma-*Bob,*" if you prefer) has often been commented on, conveniently eliminating the necessity for winding a spring or pushing a button to turn on the electricity.

Now let us turn to some other phases of music. I recall hearing that a 65 percent majority for a presidential candidate is practically a landslide. Sixty-five percent of the right notes in a musical performance is not too convincing. Take the first two measures of the melody of *America* in G:

Play correctly:

No matter how well the three G's and two A's are played, one sour tone (where F♯ is called for) will kill the entire effect, and probably the whole song! *(Play with sour F♯.)*

Music theorists, in dividing the perfect octave in half, obtain a very imperfect and unstable interval, the tritone, which for a long time has held the nickname of "the devil in music." (I now leave to each of you a chief delight of the true academician, the use of Latin terminology or other means of complicating what is simple. Please *think* of the Latin name for our villain, "the devil in music.")

Viewed one way, "the devil in music" is an augmented fourth,

(Play: whose inversion is a diminished fifth,

(Play: both very imperfect intervals. Enharmonic writing only reverses the order of the intervals. In dividing the octave in half, in straddling the fence, *in trying to please everyone, the devil in music succeeds in pleasing no one.*

The nearest neighbors of the devil are the *perfect* fourth and the *perfect* fifth, and he is halfway between the tones of the *perfect* octave. *Perhaps the strain of having only* perfect *neighbors is too much for "the devil in music"!*

An interesting experiment with a violin that has been carefully tuned starts with the violinist playing the open E string and adding the first finger on the A string to get B, a perfect fourth. If this B is then played with the open D string, it is found to be unacceptable as a major sixth. *(Play: Violin*

If we tune the B to a satisfactory relationship with the open D,

then the fourth it makes with the open E is *Play: Violin*

unacceptable. Where, then, is *B* on the A string? It is several places, *according to context;* it is *not* one fixed point only, as on the piano. *We can see here the importance of fitting a tone into its context to understand it fully and to play it correctly. The moral is obvious: Be sure you have the entire* context *before judging!*

The body of a tuned violin, resting out of its case, may be felt to vibrate strongly when another violin is played, or when an orchestra plays or a choir sings. This is a sympathetic vibration to certain tones, a sort of "humming along" by the instrument. But playing the instrument oneself is more demanding. One learns that Mother Nature demands that half of 440 double vibrations be 220, not 219.5 or 220.5.

Listen as the A string is tuned first, then the E string is tuned to a smooth fifth with the A. Next the first finger stops the G string on a perfect octave below the open A string. Now the first finger will sharp its tone slightly and this sharped tone will be bowed firmly and allowed to "ring." *(Dead) (Play:*

Next the true A will be flatted slightly, bowed firmly, and allowed to "ring." (Also *Dead*)

Now the *true* A will be fingered and bowed to "ring." Listen for the resonance of the open A and E strings, the "ringing of the bells." *(Violinist plays v to get maximum resonance.)* Once more. (This is like ringing the bell with a sledgehammer at a carnival or fair.)

Mother Nature is now saying to us, "So, you *finally* got it exactly right. *Bravo!*" *This resonance or bell-ringing is her encouraging applause.*

Chapter XXIII

Some Foreign Methods

Brief consideration will be given in this chapter to five violin methods which the author observed outside the United States. A few salient points will be noted about these methods.

1. *New Violin Method using the Pentatonic Scale* by Percival Hodgson (British, pub. Boosey & Hawkes, 1933). The four books are accompanied by *Supplementary Pieces for Violin and Piano*, to be used along with the method. Book I introduces both clockwise and anticlockwise slurs of open strings, and features cross-string bowings. The supplementary pieces follow suit with slurs, and also call for changing bow across open strings.

Pizzicato on pentatonic scales and major scales is used for introducing left-hand functions, but attention is called to this method because it applies the bowing principles discussed by Mr. Hodgson in his valuable book *Motion Study and Violin Bowing* (reprinted by the American String Teachers Association). The photographs and diagrams shown in this book provide graphic examples of what actually happens in bowing various passages.

In this connection, attention is called to the *Young Violinist's Edition* series of pieces, concerti, etc., by Theodore and Alice Pashkus (Remington Records, New York City, 1953-). This worthwhile series uses recordings as models, as does Suzuki, and it also has recorded piano accompaniments. There are extensive preparatory exercises, on a phrase-by-phrase basis. For example, the first four measures of the *Accolay Concertino in A minor* are prepared by appropriate exercises for the left hand and for bowing (using graphic curves and "round" bowing as in the Hodgson works). There is also an analysis of contact, division, and speed of bow.

2. *Praktische Violinschule* by Ferdinand Küchler (Hug & Co., Zürich, Band I, Heft 1, 1914). Much text (in German) and explanation (not for children!). Based on theory and solfeggio. Starts with theory and reading practice. Explanation of three chin rests is quite up to date. Very full description of bow hold and strokes. First bowing is staccato in the middle of the bow. All fingers are introduced; much *keeping down* of fingers. All *reading* in this method. Second Violin part for teacher often. Flats and sharps introduced. Counterclockwise and clockwise bowing motions introduced on page 28. Doublestops. Folksongs and chorales are used in duet form. When something new is introduced—*Zuerst singen!* (Sing it first.) Second pattern (minor third) often causes trouble at first for many children. Good music is used. I feel sure Suzuki knew this method.

It is easy to understand why Carl Flesch recommended this method. The approach is similar to his. I found the method popular in Switzerland; it is surprisingly up to date for its age. It has some good features, but the dry, thorough Teutonic approach is not popular today in America.

At the 1963 Tanglewood String Symposium, Joseph Silverstein, concertmaster of the Boston Symphony, commented: "In looking over beginning methods I have not seen the name of any author who has ever played a season in a major symphony orchestra." Regarding conventional study material: "As far as the rhythmic involvements and the harmonic involvement of the study, they are so naïve as to offer no challenge to the students and aid in no way in their development into fine string players and fine musicians." There is great need for "these rather antiquated methods of teaching to be substantially revised."

Presumably Mr. Silverstein was not acquainted with the following method:

3. *Vioolmethode* by Louis Metz, long a violist in Amsterdam's Concertgebouw Orchestra (Broekmans & Van Poppel, Amsterdam, 1958-62). This comprehensive method aims to provide a modern violin-pedagogic foundation, *the living language of contemporary music.* In addition to the books of the method, there

are collections of "Pieces for Performance" (violin duets and solos with piano) to go along with the method books. These pieces were commissioned from twenty-two contemporary Dutch composers, to cast specific problems (recipes) into musical form. (Use of commissioned works as part of a method has also been employed by the Dofleins and Paul Rolland.) Radio recordings were made in Holland for American educational stations.

Volume I of the method includes considerable bowing technique, with the division of the bow kept visual. Tricky counting appears already in an open string part. Details such as holding the violin and bow are left to the teacher. Duets and doublestrings appear early.

The student is advised to sing before playing and to retain fingers on strings as much as possible. Whole and half steps are designated as separated and closed fingers. Arrows show high and low tones.

3/4 and 2/4, 4/4 and 3/4 are mixed in the same exercise; 5/4 is introduced on page 18. Little canons in 5/4 appear, with unequal bowings and irregular slurring.

This method fills well the need for training young orchestra players to play contemporary rhythms, etc. How much appeal it will have for youngsters is another matter. Needless to say, Metz has not had the experience with children that Suzuki has! This is a good and valuable method and idea, just the same.

4. *The Doflein Method* by Erich and Elma Doflein. (Original in German; Schott—Associated Music Publishers; English edition in 5 vols., 1957). A course of violin instruction combined with musical theory and practice in duet-playing, it serves as an introduction to good music in all its variety. It aims "to offer the beginner a treasury of genuine and valuable material for playing, such as has not been offered before."

Bartók, Hindemith, Orff, and others represent the present period. Many works were commissioned for this method.

Volume I starts with music with five notes; the keynote is always identified. "D and A strings are singable in pitch." The fourth finger is used from the beginning, as is the whole bow. The fingerings progress rapidly—this method goes fast. There are clapping exercises. Doublenotes appear early. Harmony of fourths and fifths comes on page 21. Bartók duets are found on pages 12, 16, 23, 24. Hindemith appears on page 24, Orff on page 39. On page 40, an Orff piece uses 2/4 3/4 5/4. The minor mode comes on page 58. There is much theory in this book. Real composers, not flunkies, are featured.

The wealth of material provides a good preparation for contemporary styles. The rate of progression is so fast that supplementary material is needed. This method probably seems better to adults than to children. While the German edition was the most popular method in Germany during our visits, children were not studying violin much there. The theory and history were all good, the music very good, but no swarms of children were after it! Suzuki has loads of children studying violin and playing it well, while many others have theories and logic, but not much results to show.

5. *Suzuki Violin School,* ten volumes, plus some supplementary ones, by Shinichi Suzuki. First published by Zen-On in Tokyo, the early edition was in Japanese, with titles of pieces in German, English, and Italian, and some "pidgin English" text which was almost as difficult to decipher as the Japanese (for a westerner).

Once while my wife and I were eating in a café on the waterfront in Villefranche (French Riviera), I overheard Madame in the rear ask our waitress what language we spoke. The reply was "international." Truly, the language of the early Suzuki books was international, but fortunately, the music was all in English! There were small plastic records of explanation and performance in the jackets of the music books. These served as models for the pieces, which were to be learned by ear.

Undergoing several transformations through the years, the Suzuki Violin School is now being issued in an English edition by the Summy-Birchard Company, Evanston, Illinois. At the time of this writing, the first six volumes and recordings are available, with the remainder on the way. Summy-Birchard is also undertaking publication of a quarterly *Suzuki Journal,* the first issue to appear in early 1973.

The Suzuki Method for starting young children on violin is entirely by ear for a considerable time. Volume I contains explanations and photographs, rhythmic and tonalization exercises, and the following pieces in the key of A: *Twinkle, Twinkle, Little Star* (four variations and the theme); *Lightly Row; Song of the Wind; Go Tell Aunt Rhody; O Come, Little Children; May Song; Long, Long Ago; Allegro; Perpetual Motion;* and *Variation.* The fourth finger and key of D are then introduced and two new pieces in D: *Allegretto* and *Andantino.* Next comes the key of G in two octaves, and new pieces in G: *Étude* and *Variation;* three Bach *Minuets, The Happy Farmer,* and Gossec's *Gavotte.*

Tone, style, and the fundamentals are all stressed. This method is certainly not aimed at contemporary music for orchestra, and Mr. Suzuki is not a symphony violinist, but thousands of children have learned to play under his leadership. How about combining Suzuki with the best features of the reading methods?

With the appearance of cello, piano, viola and bass, flute (etc.) books following the Suzuki Violin School, it would seem that the method is now going through stages similar to those of Paul Herfurth's *Tune a Day. Tune a Day* achieved success as a violin method, then was issued for the other strings (but not well coordinated with the violin books), and eventually appeared for wind instruments. This process may be called "making hay while the sun shines," "striking while the iron is hot," or "panning as long as any gold shows up."

Chapter XXIV

Interlude IV: Scandinavian Saga

Our six weeks in Scandinavia during the summer of 1966 were largely spent in sightseeing, but a musician never gets entirely away from music. In Copenhagen I visited the Royal Danish Conservatory, admired Grundtvig's church with its huge, organ-like facade, shopped at Wilhelm Hansen's music store, and attended a concert in the Tivoli Concert Hall given by the local symphony. The program included works by Carl Nielsen (*Overture to Mascarade*) and Rued Langgaard (*Symphony No. 6*). Nielsen is now well established as Denmark's leading composer. As a veteran cigar smoker myself, I was pleased to note that the Danish women were great cigar smokers. And it's true what they say about those Danish books!

Bergen, Norway, has an Ole Bull Plaza near the Norge Hotel, with a statue of the violinist in action and one of the fairy sprite who teaches how to play violin. Did you know the violin is taught by fairies? (In Denmark, two buses of fairies made a Fairytale Tour to the Hans Christian Andersen house and museum in Odense.) At the Krage store in Bergen I bought a miniature Hardanger fiddle—more about this later.

A few miles out of Bergen, on a knoll overlooking water and woods, is Troldhaugen ("Hill of the Sprites"), summer home of Edvard and Nina Grieg. Their graves are in the side of a cliff here. Having a longstanding affinity for the melodious and harmonically charming music of Grieg, I enjoyed very much visiting this beautiful spot. I did, however, make a serious error at Troldhaugen!

Knowing that Grieg had a studio-hut built near his home where he worked in solitude, I mistook a quite small building nearby for this hut. It was *not!* It was a *de*composition hut—the true composition hut was much larger and better furnished, at the end of a long path, and down by the water.

Driving along the Hardangerfjord, where Grieg lived for a year, hearing the Hardanger fiddles played for folk dancing, and listening to records of expert players of the instrument reminded me that the Hardanger fiddle sounds much like a bagpipe. A guide suggested that may be why the Vikings left! At any rate, this instrument often has a devil's head on its scroll, and is so devilish that its player is not allowed in church at weddings.

Tuned in fifths except for the bottom string, with a flat bridge and old-style bow, a set of sympathetic strings like those of the viol d'amore, and frequent beautiful inlay, this folk instrument is played with characteristic ornamentation and sound that had a very obvious effect on the music of Edvard Grieg.

Grieg's many spring, flower and bird pieces, Tivoli's many sun pieces, etc., the university students' spring celebrations (throwing caps in the air and other Rites of Spring), all show the pleasure when the long Scandinavian winter is over. This is understandable!

FFFFF in Norway does not mean extremely loud, but is a short course in Norwegian words: Fjord = inlet (there's a Fjord in your future); Fisk = fish; Fonn = glacier; Foss = waterfall; Fjell = mountain. We discovered that Norwegian children learn to ski at three years of age—a form of Talent Education. Also in Norway, the many huge boulders that dot the mountainsides are trolls that didn't get in on time at night, and so were changed to rocks. The trolls were certainly a tardy and numerous people!

After seeing many Handelsbanken in Oslo, one can imagine Georg Friedrich coming out, standing in the doorway and saying to himself, "Boy, am I baroque!" When we saw Vigeland's famed sculptures in Frogner Park, we decided that the dominating column (Mankind Struggling) could be called "Getting ahead at Oberlin" or "Changing seats on our bus."

Driving through Varmland in Sweden recalled a favorite folksong, *Ack Värmeland, du sköna.* In Uppsala we visited the university, cathedral and Dag Hammerskjöld's grave, then went on to see swarms of beatniks in Stockholm.

We attended a service and organ program in St. Clara Cathedral, found the Carl Milles Garden quite interesting, and went to Skansen for folk dancing at the Midsummer celebration. The colorful entrance procession of the folk dancers was led by a sturdy marching orchestra of fiddlers, reminding me somewhat of a section of *Peter and the Wolf*: "Imagine the triumphant procession. . . ."

An eighteen-hour ride on a Finnish steamer from Stockholm to Helsinki took us through Swedish and Finnish archipelagos of some seventy thousand islands and the Baltic Sea. Finland reminded us of the Upper Peninsula of Michigan, where we have spent many summers. The remainder of this chapter is taken from notes I prepared for a program, "Finland and Northern Michigan."

Rocky shores, clear, cold water, vast forests—the refreshing music of the waves lapping the shore and the wind blowing through huge pine trees—have long been dear to my heart. Scandinavians in large numbers have settled in Michigan's Upper Peninsula, which bears striking resemblance to their homelands. I have enjoyed the friendship of many of these people through the years.

Suomi Kutsuu (Finland Calling), from the television station in Marquette, Michigan, on Sunday mornings is said to be the only Finnish-language regular program in the United States. There is also a Suomi College in Hancock, Michigan. Conducting several string workshops in the Negaunee-Ishpeming-Marquette area provided an opportunity to become acquainted with many young Finns. I enjoyed visiting their homeland.

Utsjoki in Northern Finland had one long day of 1,752 hours (or 73 normal 24-hour days); it also had one long night of 1,224 hours (or 51 normal days). Thus, an eight-hour workday would leave much free time in both summer and winter! Lapland in Northern Scandinavia features the Midnight sun in June and July, the picturesque Lapps (only about twenty-six hundred are left in Finland, but one owns five thousand reindeer), cold water, and tundra. The pleasure coming when the long winter is *over* is universal in Scandinavia! (Also in Michigan, despite the many snowmobiles and fishing shanties on frozen lakes.)

Finland is 721 miles long and 336 miles at its greatest width, lying between the sixtieth and seventieth degrees of latitude (about one-fourth of it is above the Arctic Circle). It is larger than England, Scotland, Wales, and Ireland together. Only 10 percent of the land is cultivated, 9 percent of the country is water (sixty thousand lakes), 30 percent is marshland (Suomi, the word for Finland, means *marsh*), 38 percent is forest, the rest is hilly, tundra, or wasteland.

Of some 4,700,000 Finns, about 92 percent speak Finnish, a "double or nothing" language (in Finnish, I suppose it would be "Hankki-Paukki"), which belongs to the Finno-Ugrian group, and is related to Hungarian and Japanese. There is no gender; the same word is used for "he" and "she." (In Northern Michigan, the Finns' language is called "Finglish.")

About 8 percent speak Swedish. In Southern Finland, all town names are given in both Finnish and Swedish (Helsinki and Helsingfors; Turku and Åbo.) There is no illiteracy. About 93 percent Lutherans, the Finns have paid their debts honorably, and at considerable sacrifice. One-third of the Finns are farmers, one-fifth industrial workers. Woodworking and papermaking are the leading industries. The largest cities are Helsinki (500,000); Tampere (Tammerfors) (140,000); Turku (139,000); and Oulu (Uleåborg) (80,000).

Long dominated by Sweden, then Russia, Finland was in 1917 declared a free and independent state. It was one of the first countries to introduce the eight-hour workday, and was the first country in Europe to grant women equal political rights (1906). Many women were in the Finnish government—three women ministers in the cabinet, forty-three women members in parliament (about one-fourth of the total). Three-fourths of the dentists, 40 percent of pharmacists, 30 percent of doctors and architects were women. But the women were *feminine*, not interested in burning bras or in unisex!

Important in Finland are music (Jean Sibelius outstanding), fine arts, industrial design, handicrafts, and architecture. (The A-Frame design originated in Scandinavia and is used in many churches and other buildings. It is a good roof style for coping with much snow. The Finns are masters at blending their buildings into natural surroundings.)

Finnish architect Eliel Saarinen (1873-1950) designed the Helsinki Railway Station and many other buildings in Finland, then came to America and designed the Boston Symphony's Concert Shed, Theater-Concert Hall, and Chamber Music Buildings at Tanglewood; Kleinhans Music Hall in Buffalo, and outstanding American skyscrapers. His son Eero Saarinen of Cranbrook Institute, Bloomfield Hills, Michigan, became one of America's leading architects.

In the Kaupunginhotelli, Tampere, Finland, we had a bathroom where one could sit on the toilet, brush his teeth, and take a shower simultaneously—really efficient! We had a fine sauna bath in this hotel, three dollars for two of us. There are some 500,000 saunas in Finland, one for every nine people. (We have also had sauna baths in Northern Michigan.) Webster's Dictionary includes two Finnish words: *sauna* and *sisu*. Sisu means endurance or fortitude, such as that required to take a sauna bath at 100 degrees C., then jump into ice water or a snowbank! In Tampere we also attended the famous Pyynikkin Kesateatteri, an open-air theater with the world's first revolving stadium. After the play, the Mid-Summer Bonfire was burned on a raft in the lake.

We stayed at the Polar Hotel (which had a Polar Bar) in Rovaniemi, a town astride the Arctic Circle, designed by Alvar Aalto like reindeer antlers. Like virtually everything in Lapland, Rovaniemi is entirely new since the war, as the Germans burned the place on the way home from their unsuccessful attempt to help Finland against the Russians.

Then we set out for the North Cape, three hundred miles further north, for spectacular views of the midnight sun. We ate lots of reindeer steak, had the best whale dinner we ever had or will have, drank lakka (cloudberry liqueur), mesimarja (liqueur from the Arctic brambleberry—Finland only), and aquavit (all over Scandinavia). Good accommodations were available in Finland for seven to nine dollars, including meals.

We paid our tribute to Jean Sibelius (1865-1957) in his native *Finlandia* country—Aulanko, Hämeenlinna (statue in a park, plaque on the school he attended; museum in birthplace includes photo of Piano Trio including Sibelius and his brother, with the Sanctus Serafin violin Sibelius played now kept under glass). At Ainola (Jarvenpaa) his widow Aino and one of their six daughters were still living. Sibelius is buried on the grounds of this home he loved so much. Our guide told us that once a group of schoolchildren prepared some songs and came to Ainola. Sibelius said, "Let me look at them, *but don't let them sing!*" He was very sensitive and self-centered. He hated the dentist's drill; his dentist and office girl dreaded to see his appointment come and watched the road with apprehension, to see Sibelius coming for his appointment. It's quite a switch for a patient to scare a dentist—Sibelius must have been truly *formidable!*

Tapiola, his last major work, was written in 1925 (his last composition date shows 1929). About thirty unproductive years at the end of his life show good critical judgment and are nothing to be ashamed of. Unfortunately, many musicians go on performing or composing after they "have had it," as everyone knows but themselves.

In Northern Michigan I have worked with many Finnish string players from six months old through high school age and found them a pleasure to teach, sensitive, courteous, and attentive. The woodworking in the North includes some violinmaking. The Michigan Finns are amused by the "Black Power" or quota concept. They, as a minority group, also have bumper stickers: Finn Power, Finn-Dago Power, etc.

In the *Detroit Free Press* for September 27, 1970, travel editor Arthur Juntunen wrote in an article about his recent trip to Finland:

> On a sightseeing bus, someone asked Sinikka, the cute Lapp hostess with large brown eyes, what the Lapps do in summer.
> "We fish and make love," she replied.
> "And what do you do in winter?"
> "Well, we just don't fish."

Old John, my fishing guide in Northern Michigan about thirty-five years ago, told me the same thing (in plainer words) about life in the Upper Peninsula. So, the Old and New are really *One World!* As the French say, "C'est la même chose."

Chapter XXV

Bowing

Many books and articles have been written on bowing, and thousands of bowing exercises for students have been written or prescribed. I do not wish to repeat what I have written on this subject in my two earlier books, but will add a few thoughts or suggestions.

Franz Kneisel: "To play with real beauty of expression, the bow supplies the only true key. All real art begins with phrasing and this too lies altogether in the mastery of the bow, the very soul of the violin."

Several practice techniques are used to insure that some phrasing-break or "luft-pause" occurs in a student's playing. The bow may continue on beyond the string at phrase endings, make a circle and return to start the next phrase. Or both arms may be extended, with the violin left in place. Or, as Paul Rolland does it, the violin may be carried away as both arms are extended. In all these exercises, a break in the sound is forced. Then everything is left in place, but a similar breathing pause is observed in the sound. Suzuki writes, "In Volume 3, particular emphasis should be placed on the study of phrasing. Children should learn to end each phrase pianissimo."

Emil Hauser taught a great variety of bowing strokes in terms of different vowels and consonants. He gave much attention to phrasing and its development. He wrote phrases in diminution, to compress each entire phrase into a little space and show clearly its grouping.

As with a single tone, every phrase has a beginning, a middle or duration, and an ending. While I have often felt some repulsion for the school of piano teachers who insist that music must always be getting louder or softer, mechanically making a crescendo on an ascending melodic line and a diminuendo on a descending line, I must admit that they get some variety in performance. I have often heard children play violin at a steady mf level—like a table top, or "going nowhere on a monotonous road." On the other hand, does music *always* have to be "going somewhere"?

In his *Forty Easy Variations* for Violin or Cello, with Piano accompaniment, employing various styles of bowing, Opus 3 (1901), Ottokar Sevick shows another side of his teaching genius than the dry technical analysis usually associated with his name. With more than one hundred variants, these are very musical little pieces with effective piano accompaniments—which could be used as solos. Involving major and minor keys through five sharps and six flats, and the first few positions, the left hand is kept relatively easy most of the time. All parts of the bow and all basic strokes are developed, and a great variety of rhythms, patterns, and string crossings are introduced. "Flying" and standing bowings, many off-string bowings, dynamic changes—all make this a very valuable bow-study book. Titles for variations, such as Mazurka, Siciliana, Walzer, Marcia funebre, suggest that these studies are more musical than most such works. I'm not sure that "easy" is the right word for everything in the book, however!

In 1911 Carl Flesch published the English version of his dry, didactic *Urstudien*, which broke bowing down into six primary movements and emphasized finger movement. Flesch later disavowed finger movement as a separate feature in bowing. (He was a big enough man to admit a mistake, as when he forgot while soloing with orchestra, stopped, and said "It's my fault.") The six primary movements defined by Flesch were used by Harold Berkley in his books on bowing which came out in the 1940s.

Ivan Galamian calls Lucien Capet "a strong influence on me musically and pedagogically." Shinichi Suzuki tells of the deep impression made on him when he heard the Capet Quartet. Nineteen sixteen marked the appearance of Capet's monumental work on bowing, *La Technique Supérieure de l'Archet*, in French and never translated, as far as I know.

Capet was an idealist and mystic:

Technic of the left hand is the *letter,* of the right hand, the spirit. *La Beauté n'a pas besoin de nous, mais nous avons besoin d'Elle.* We are walled in by great pride with our limited knowledge, and so cannot discover the truths outside ourselves. Our dignity grows as our pride diminishes and we discover joy outside ourselves. The true role of the artist is to identify himself with beauty and not to attract the attention of his contemporaries. Complete identification with beauty means loss of self-consciousness. The ideal grows as we perfect ourselves.

Capet's book on bowing is in two parts. Part I explains principles and Part II consists of practical exercises based on the principles. Space permits listing only a few ideas from this exhaustive work.

The ring finger is the "spiritual guide" in the sensitivity of the fingers on the stick. Beauty is the central concern.

Horizontal movement has the little finger pushing the stick towards the fingerboard, while the first finger pulls the stick toward the bridge. This is used to play loud at the point, for example.

Vertical movement may be practiced by alternate leaning of the first and little fingers down on the stick (making a semicircle with the thumb and long finger as the fulcrum). At the frog, the thumb and first two fingers sustain the bow, while the last two lean down on it.

Much emphasis is given to bow divisions—equal divisions first, then unequal (balanced by the sensitivity of the bow-fingering, in the horizontal movement). Nuances are to be obtained by pressure of fingers, and rarely by movement of bow on string (Flesch: too great insistence on this; Suzuki: change dynamics first by amount of bow used).

Roulé (rolling the stick in the fingers) is advised for strong passages and developing the sensitivity of the fingers. *Suppress vibrato* appears often—don't rely on the left hand only for expression. Capet has all doublestops arranged according to which string should be favored with more weight.

Détaché is masculine (rock, fire); *lié* is feminine (water, air). Slurred *lié* should have "all the moods of the ocean," and *louré* he calls "coup ondulé." The wave action is good for describing the bow motion in this latter stroke.

Practice open and stopped tones to get the same sound. Suzuki expresses this idea thus: "Open string second finger." I suppose that since the ideal test for a smooth bow change is achieved when the ear cannot tell when it occurs, the ideal should also be that the ear cannot tell whether an open or stopped tone is played. Or perhaps, since an "open" string is actually stopped at both ends by wood, we need *wooden fingers* to emulate this sound. Some teachers prefer to avoid open strings whenever possible, but then you have to tune the lowest string below its written pitch!

Sautillé à la corde, sautillé rebondissant, various spiccatos are all discussed and exercised. *Coup lancé* is the most rapid stroke, with full bow used. All the bowings are practiced on scales and exercises, etc., *not* on music.

Contact points and speed are hardly discussed or practiced at all, showing the incompleteness of the view at the time (1916). More recent bowing studies make much of these neglected factors. Samuel Applebaum, for example, gives the following advice:

When to Play near Fingerboard

1. Long notes that are soft
2. Short notes that are soft (wrist and finger, "eraser")
3. Short notes that are loud
4. Martelé strokes
5. Spiccato strokes
6. Sautillé strokes
7. Ricochet strokes
8. Three- and four-voice chords that are short
9. All sforzando attacks

When to Play near Bridge

1. Long notes that are loud
2. Three- and four-voice chords that are sustained (start chord near fingerboard, but sustain it near bridge)

3. All above-mentioned bowings that are played near the fingerboard, are played near the bridge when above the fifth position

Applebaum has a two-album set of records called *The String Bowings* put out by Golden Crest Records, Inc. His *Orchestral Bowing Études,* for all string instruments, are published by Belwin (1965).

Attention is called to *Manual of Orchestral Bowing* by Charles Gigante (unpublished thesis, Eastman School of Music, 1953) and to *Violinist's Guide to Orchestral Playing* by William Nowinski (C. Fischer, 1961). *Dictionary of Bowing Terms* by Joel Berman and Barbara Seagrave was published by American String Teachers Association in 1968. A number of Paul Rolland's valuable films on bowing are now available from Theodore Presser Co.

Modern virtuosi give advice on bowing. Isaac Stern: The bow arm "hangs." Arthur Grumiaux: "Carry the bow." Mischa Elman: The *thumb* is most important in bowing.

In my own teaching of string classes I found these bowing tests useful: 1. *Dictation* (on the D major scale)—I played various bowings; students notated and marked the bowings I played; 2. *Marking bowings* for passages with no bowing indications.

Chapter XXVI

All Gall, in Three Parts

I. *Flit to Florida* (1969-70)

Mrs. Cook and I were a pair of "migrating snowbirds" in the first winter after I joined the Melon Club at my retirement (in this club, one's wife says *"Honey do* this. *Honey do* that.")

Quartered in a small efficiency apartment in Port Richey, in the "Suncoast Section" of Florida, we looked out on a tidal river. My two favorite songs soon became "By a Bend in the River" and "Way Down Upon the Pithlachascotee River." From our dining table we saw palm trees, ripe oranges, grapefruit and kumquat may, as we enjoyed the variations sung by a mockingbird. It was an ideal location for writing my Suzuki book, although my little Cutlass looked out of place in the row of Caddies in our parking spaces. Neighbor Charley said he paid eight thousand dollars for his; I said "I didn't pay that much for my car." (Many Caddie owners who have barely finished eighth grade have an obvious disdain for the academic profession.)

We drove to Tampa to see the Luminary (Spanish) in Carrolwood on Christmas Eve and to attend an interesting program on the Christmas Star at the planetarium of the University of South Florida. We witnessed the Gasparilla pirates' invasion of Tampa, and noted that in the subsequent parade Colonel Sanders on his "Kentucky Fried Chicken" float got a bigger hand than Governor Kirk or any other politician. Mayor Greco of Tampa, after surrendering the city to the Gasparilla pirates, told them: "If you give back some of our women, you can have the potholes, pollution, and the unions!"

We admired the George Inness, Jr., paintings in a small Universalist Church in Tarpon Springs, where we had delicious Greek salad and seafood at Pappas' Restaurant. We had other good meals on our trip at the Golden Lamb in Lebanon, Ohio;

Boone Tavern in Berea, Kentucky; and in Florida at the Kapok Tree Inn near Clearwater, Oyster Bar in Sarasota, Aunt Hatties' in St. Petersburg, Columbia (Spanish) in Orlando, and Bern's Steak House in Tampa. A sign in a Clearwater Steak House proclaimed, very truthfully: "At the price of bacon now, hogs are living pretty high on the people." However, the breakfast menu of a bakery-restaurant in New Port Richey listed: SPECIAL: Three hen-pecked eggs, bacon etc., 59¢ (also known as the Gambler's choice—best two out of three).

Many "Snowbird Specials" were offered, in which the advertised price and the true price varied considerably. For instance, a new house priced $6,990 didn't include the doors, windows, and a few other minor details (like the price of a new car which doesn't include engine, wheels, etc.).

During three nights in a row in January, the temperature dropped to freezing and only went up to fifty degrees in the daytime. Stunned fish of many kinds were floating on top of the water, including Snook up to fifteen or twenty pounds. This inspired me to write our grandchildren: COOK LOOK SNOOK; COOK SNOOK LOOK; LOOK COOK, SNOOK! LOOK SNOOK, COOK! SNOOK COOK LOOK; SNOOK LOOK COOK! My wife then sang "It is enough!" (without cello obbligato).

In February I gave a program for music teachers in Tampa area schools. In their business session they discussed a "behavioral procedures" form for each class and organization taught during the week, to be filled out in triplicate by every teacher and sent to the State Department of Education. A resolution was passed unanimously to invite the State Music Supervisor to come and explain details of the form to teachers, who couldn't figure them out (I couldn't, either). *It was good to hear Pedaguese again!* I heard about the first-grader in a disadvantaged school who, when the teacher was relating the story of Little Red Riding Hood and came to the part played by the Wolf, blurted out "The S.O.B.!"

We visited a music teacher whose two daughters had recently graduated in woodwinds from Oberlin Conservatory. The father reported that neither daughter wanted to be in a symphony orchestra to "play for capitalists"! A St. Petersburg Junior College student pontificated: "Serious (classical) music is dead." The Dean of Tampa University, after flunking out one hundred and fifty students, explained: "We don't want students whose major is Clearwater Beach and guitar!" When I had visited New College in Sarasota (on Parents' Day, as it turned out) and was returning to my car in the parking lot, I found all four tires flat on car after car. Fortunately, I reached mine before the group of yippy students had given me their "Official Welcome."

A few musical notes made while in Florida follow: Young Uck Kim, twenty-two years old, soloed with the Gulf Coast Symphony. The Cologne Chamber Orchestra had a Japanese concertmaster and soloist. Suzuko Hillyer explained intelligently the flood of violinists now coming from the Orient. The Jacksonville and Mobile symphonies disbanded in midseason, and Kansas City was very late in opening. The London Symphony Summer Festival at Daytona Beach was canceled, with money still owed the orchestra for the last summer. This year rock groups will be used, to try to recoup some of the big deficit incurred, even with the orchestra's schedule of mini-rehearsals and maxi-performances. (This sounded similar to Blossom Center, where Tiny Tim was advertised to "tiptoe through the tulips"). The London solo cellist was coming to teach at the University of South Florida, joining the many "orchestra dropouts," even concertmasters and other first-chair men from domestic and foreign orchestras, now found in academic institutions all over the United States, despite their great love for orchestral playing, deep concern for the plight of the orchestras, and worry about the quality of their replacements.

In March, a program at the University of South Florida introduced me to a school only ten years old, but with fifteen thousand students. The campus buildings were designed by Frank Lloyd Wright. "Innovation and Excellence" was the school's motto. I was interested to learn that Dr. Max Kaplan, Director, Institute for Studies of Leisure (also a violinist in the Gulf Coast Symphony), was said to spend much time lying in a hammock—he *practices what he teaches!*

When neighbor Sayer appeared in a Harvard sweatshirt, I asked if that was his alma mater. No, it was surplus equipment from his store, he was a graduate of Knox College ("Hard Knocks"). Many neighbors went to St. Pete for the opening of the Ringling Circus tour (where the television show was filmed). But already at Jacksonville, the Flying Zacchinis were squashed!

Route 19 carried such a congestion of traffic that it was called "Suicide Trail." Waiting in a barbershop one day, I listened to an elderly gentleman explain how he played *Florida Roulette* when he entered Route 19 from Moog Road, where he lived: "I let six cars pass, then go." After he had departed, a highway patrolman in civvies, waiting in the barbershop, announced: "I'll take a look at that intersection." The Florida Highway Patrol conducted a week's campaign which they labeled "Courteous Intimidation."

On a trip to Sanibel and Captiva islands, we found Fort Myers hit by a rain- and windstorm, with many big palm fronds down in the streets. A frond in need is a frond indeed, but one can have too many fronds at times. My attitude was positively unfrondly when one came down on my car! In Florida, a twin bill that plays throughout the year is "Falling Leaves" and "The Rake's Progress."

We learned some things at the Thomas Edison winter home and laboratory in Fort Myers. Tired of slurs on Florida beef, he once served a dinner party shoe leather called "Western beef." After they had chewed for a while, he gave them some "Florida beef." As a joke, Henry Ford sent Edison a blank stone for the Memory Walk in his garden. Edison's comment: "Henry couldn't afford to have his name put on it." Edison married an Akron girl, saying, "Anyone with nerve enough to play piano in public as badly as she did, attracted his attention!" Edison had absolute memory (total recall)—he didn't label the contents of hundreds of bottles, etc., in his laboratory, which reminded my wife of my study.

We read that thirty-five hundred people per week were moving to Florida. A friend advised checking for citrus trees, not cypress, on Florida property *before* you buy. We saw a septic tank put down into water beside one new house, reminding me of the admonition, "When you take a drink keep your teeth together."

Evening entertainment in Florida includes greyhound races. My neighbor Charley went to the track at St. Pete one night, bet on a beautiful dog, and saw this dog easily out-distance the pack. Suddenly, when only a few feet from the finish line, the dog stopped and did his business, as all the other dogs went by. Charley said the roar from the stands could be heard across the Gulf of Mexico!

As Lady Godiva, who was not ashamed of her Unaccompanied Bach (or Frond, either), said near the end of her famous ride: "Now I approach my close." Our only regret about our Flit to Florida was that we came back about a month too soon.

II. *Tour to Tuscon* (1971)

My notes and comments on this winter trip during January, February, and March make a book in themselves. So, reluctantly, I'll have to cut them down to cover only the musical part, and that rather sketchily.

At Valparaiso University, Indiana, I did a string clinic for Professor Philip Gehring and his wife Betty Burns, and discovered that Professor Fred Telschow, then head of the Music Department, had studied with me in the summer of 1953. When I suggested that we play the rhythm of Valparaiso Indiana

♫♫♫ ♫♫♫ some youngsters informed me that they were from

Hobart. So we played their rhythm (Indiana Hobart ♫♫♫ ♫)

on Suzuki's first variation.

There was an evening recital by Japanese violinist Mari Tsumura in the beautiful Resurrection Chapel. At the reception afterward, I noted that she didn't understand English, when convenient not to. This phenomenon occurs frequently, I have found through the years. At least, we Americans are consistent in *never* understanding Japanese.

At the University of Illinois in Urbana we visited a friend of long standing, Professor Paul Rolland. His *String Research Project,* backed by a government grant from 1967 to 1970, is a remarkable achievement. I heard a select group of about eighteen youngsters play some of the pieces from their recent appearance at the White House Conference on Children and work on some Bartók Duets they were to play for ASTA in March. I agree with the critic who wrote that they "demonstrated an exciting and obviously enjoyable approach to learning strings through active bodily movement and the use of contemporary music." The Project is titled *The Teaching of Action in String Playing.*

We saw some of the excellent series of color films produced by the project, and now available from Theodore Presser Co. The accompanying manuals are to appear in book form soon. Attention is also called to *Prelude to String Teaching* by Paul Rolland, Margaret Rowell, and Edward Krolick (Boosey and Hawkes), and *New Tunes for Strings* by Stanley Fletcher, vols. I & 2 (Presser).

For the latest information on any phase of *The Teaching of Action in String Playing,* send inquiry to String Instrument Research, 404 E. Oregon St., Urbana, Ill. 61801. All string teachers will find Professor Rolland's project a veritable mine of useful ideas, techniques, and music. Paul is a man who never stops learning and growing!

We visited the impressive Krannert Center for the Performing Arts, a $25 million complex dedicated in April, 1969, consisting of four halls and an outdoor amphitheater, all with a huge common lobby. I was pleased to learn that the old frame building at I.U., known for many years as the "String Annex," was soon to be abandoned in favor of a new music building. (A nonacademic nephew seemed to enjoy informing me that at Edwardsville "The University is built around the String Annex" —an old farmhouse off by itself.)

In Decatur we visited our friends, Mr. and Mrs. George Nagy, both good violin teachers. Seeing Rolland and Nagy reminded me of how much Hungarians have contributed to music, and to violin playing in particular.

We attended a lecture-recital at Millikin University given by Vladimir Ussachevsky on electronic music. His most effective examples were of comedy and film-accompaniment.

In Godfrey we visited former students, Professor and Mrs. Burt Harbison, and heard a violin recital by Jaime Laredo at Monticello College. In St. Louis we saw Ma-chan and Eiko Kataoka (both now playing in the Symphony), and had our first glimpse of their baby Chizu—a doll!

At Southern Illinois University (Carbondale) I lectured on Suzuki, had a good visit with my old friend, Professor John Wharton and his wife, and was impressed by John's introduction of me at Altgeld Hall: "These little Japanese children play better than any undergraduate S.I.U. ever had!" The Old Main building had been burned down by students in June; the Music-Administration building had been burned at Valparaiso U,; I wondered just how many college buildings had burned down over the country. Crumby-looking students, lying around on the floor in student centers in many schools, with a glazed stare on their faces, are not a very inspiring sight! However, a student's question at my lecture—"Is Suzuki Talent Education like teaching a blind person?"—was quite perceptive.

Visiting Mrs. Norma Jean Seaton and her family in Parsons, Kansas, was like a breath of fresh air in a polluted atmosphere. Clean air and water, an enthusiastic Suzuki Parents Association whose float and marching children with violins won several parade prizes—all were refreshing. About sixty Suzuki children— the girls in white blouses and red jumpers, boys wearing white shirts, black bow ties, and red vests—played for us Sunday afternoon. At church in the morning, young Laura Seaton wrote down the notes for *The Happy Farmer* for me, after I had done the same for *Minuetto Two*.

We detoured a bit to the Will Rogers Memorial in Claremore, Oklahoma. A tape of Will speaking still gave me a lift—his optimism and gentle, chuckling humor are badly needed today.

On the attractive campus of the University of Tulsa, we visited several friends. Professor Aldo Mancinelli of the piano faculty told his director, William McKee (French horn teacher), that he had played horn in the Training Orchestra which I had conducted at Oberlin many years ago. (Another fine pianist, Professor Howard Karp of the University of Illinois, had played cello in that orchestra.) I believe these hot-shot pianists rather fancied the idea that they also played another instrument! Mancinelli was soon to solo with the Dallas Symphony and at the Alaska Festival in May. An eighteen-year-old freshman, Joseph Ries, played a movement of the Brahms D minor Piano Concerto for us, an excellent sample of Mancinelli's teaching.

We also had pleasant visits with two long-time friends, Professor John Toms of the Tulsa voice faculty, and Professor Louise Waldorf, head of music in the Oklahoma College of Liberal Arts, Chickasha, and violinist in the Oklahoma City Symphony. We learned that the concertmaster of this orchestra was Kenji Kobayashi, a fine Suzuki graduate whom we had met in Japan in 1963.

In Albuquerque, New Mexico, we spent several days attending the Convention of the MENC Southwestern Division at the University of New Mexico. Popejoy Hall and other facilities were good, but not always equaled by personnel and performance. We heard the Albuquerque Youth Symphony, a large group, under Dale Kempter; the Amarillo High School Orchestra featuring its concertmistress playing a small violin lightly in part of the Saint-Saëns Concerto, and Penderecki's *Threnody* for fifty-two strings —effective, but too long. (Merle Isaac said publicly that he thought the second violins were out of tune in one spot—no laughs; his joke went over like a lead balloon.) Samuel Applebaum did some sight-reading with this orchestra. I wondered how many thousands of such affairs Sam had done through the years?

The Texas Tech University Symphony under Paul Ellsworth played a program of five overtures. The large group played well, but needed more first violins. It was good to see Robert Deahl, assistant dean, and Richard Meek, bassoon teacher, both friends from Oberlin days. I found cellist Georges Miquelle looking fine, retired and living in Albuquerque. When I asked about Mischa Mischakoff he told me, then added "Mischa can't quit!" We enjoyed a pleasant Mexican dinner in La Placita, Old Town Plaza.

Howard Hanson, seventy-five then, gave one of his typical talks about the musical state of the nation. He allowed that the "cultural explosion" in music so far had been mainly in the field of architecture. (Isaac Stern: Our "Edifice Complex.") The Hanson Night of his compositions made me think almost everything was the "Romantic" Symphony—one long Interlochen theme. At the end he was given a big Western hat, promptly said "I always wanted one," and rode off into the sunset like a born cowboy.

El Paso, Texas, brought reunions with old friends—Eugene Adams was still playing in the Symphony, but had retired from teaching in the public schools. His conductor said he was glad Gene was out of music education, "that massacre of good music." When Adams talked about Jewish tone in violin playing, he sounded just the same as he had years ago when he was playing in the Cleveland Orchestra, long before *Fiddler on the Roof!*

It was a time of double crisis in El Paso: *Hair* in the public schools, and dismissal of first oboe in the Symphony (on stage at a concert, yet). We enjoyed an excellent steak dinner and very pleasant evening in the home of George Webber and Milan Svambera, two first-class string and orchestra teachers in the El Paso school system, and friends of long standing. Of course, the old Prof had to take a test on entering the house, where the hi-fi was on. What composition was being played? I guessed wrong—it was Joachim's *Hungarian Concerto,* played by Charles Treger and the Louisville Symphony. At least I could tell these two young perpetrators of a Spanish Inquisition that I had long had this music, but had never heard it performed before.

And so it came to pass that on February 1 we arrived at the Dream House Motel in Tucson, "The Old Pueblo," where we were to spend the next two months. Dr. Max Ervin and his wife Jane, both Oberlin graduates, welcomed us. Dr. Ervin is Director of Music for the Tucson Public Schools and Jane is a very competent violinist. Soon we met Ray Van Dienst, State Director of Music with his office in Phoenix.

We heard one of Herbert Levinson's violin recitals in his series of three, covering the ten Beethoven sonatas. Each recital was given in a different location, a popular procedure today. A concert by the Youth Orchestra of the Tucson Symphony under James Stevenson produced, in the *Carnival of the Animals,* what Dr. Ervin called "the only transposing Cuckoo he has ever heard."

We discovered that Dr. Paul Van Bodegraven had chosen Tucson for his retirement home with his wife, Fran. He did not miss the headaches connected with running the Music Department in New York University. Dr. Allen McHose, wintering in Tucson, felt the same way about retirement from his responsibilities at the Eastman School of Music. I enjoyed hearing his reminiscences, such as, when a student he was always adding ninths to Foote and Spaulding, but his teacher wouldn't allow him to get away with it! One of the greatest pleasures in retirement is that there is time for relaxed visiting, with no guilty feeling that one should be practicing, grading papers, or preparing for tomorrow's schedule.

At a concert by the University of Arizona Orchestra under Henry Johnson, pianist Claudio Arrau played the Grieg *Concerto* and Weber *Concert Piece.* The conductor, whom I had known in Chicago long ago, told me that the indestructible Rudolph Ganz had visited Tucson at the age of ninety-three.

On February 12 I did a workshop session with Miss Yvonne Tait's Suzuki students, many of them only two years old. Miss Tait's warm, motherly manner was reflected in the obvious love the children showed for her. Hot, dry weather made tuning the biggest problem for strings, she said. Later that day I heard a program given at a junior high school by the Tucson String Teachers' Ensemble. They play in various schools every Friday afternoon, on the theory that it is good for children to hear their teachers play, teachers keep up their playing, and rapport and communication among teachers are improved.

With our friends, Mr. and Mrs. Carl Bacon, we attended the Folk Mass in Saint Philip's In The Hills Church, beautiful with striking picture windows looking out on the desert and mountain. I was amused to see rooms marked "Adams" and "Eves," thought of a church in Charleston, S.C., whose bulletin board read "Come in and get your faith lifted," and cast my vote in favor of some humor in churches.

The Folk Mass is a good example of Talent Education. A soloist sings a line, then the congregation repeats it, by ear of course. This is dance music, with a beat. The only fault I found was that the congregation should have been in the aisles doing their thing, not sitting in the pews in a prayerful attitude.

An all-German concert by the Koeckert Quartet, with father and son on violins, showed real precision and unanimity. Leonid Kogan's violin recital was picketed by students, protesting Russia's treatment of Jews. Kogan's family was reported under house arrest until his return to Russia, to insure against his defection. In sonatas by Brahms, Bach, Franck, and Tartini-Kreisler, Kogan was a first-rate violinist, with everything completely under control.

At one of the free Sunday Evening Forums given in the University auditorium, Ballet America gave a very enjoyable performance of Burch Mann's *"Big Country."* When I went to Max Ervin's office to judge students competing for Interlochen scholarships, I noted the sign outside his office, "Nutcracker Suite," and two signs on his desk: "Office mistakes are equal the sum of the squares employed" and "Diplomacy is the ability to tell a person to go to hell, in such a nice way that he looks forward to the trip." Need I say that Max is an excellent administrator? His current rate was 150 applications per job opening.

When an Audubon lecturer from up-state New York reported that their Snow Festival had recently been snowed out, we asked our cleaning maid if there was a law against bad weather in Arizona (it seemed so). She replied "Yes, just like Camelot!" Some natives secretly told us the state motto was "Dust to dust" —it's the only place I've ever been where wind, rain, and dew may have mud in them.

A visit to Mrs. Eleanor Lillich, widow of a colleague in Oberlin, in Sun City acquainted us with a booming community where eleven new modular homes were completed per day. She drove us to Camelback Inn (ninety dollars a day per person, almost like going to the hospital) and to Carefree, where all streets have names such as Easy Street, Leisure Lane, or Ho-Hum, and where a large sundial heats water for a business establishment.

Beautiful new Grady Gammage Auditorium, at Arizona State University in Tempe, was one of the last creations of Frank Lloyd Wright. Georg Szell called it "perhaps the best among the new halls in the country." Here the Phoenix Symphony under guest conductor Pierre Hetu played a concert with violinist Kyung Wha Chung as soloist in the Mendelssohn *Concerto.* She played well, making karate chops, weight shifts, digs, and high bounces for a big tone, but slowed down parts of the first movement unmercifully. Conductor Phil Spurgeon says this orchestra costs $2,700 per hour, including rehearsal time.

Igor Gorin was teaching at the University of Arizona. His recital there drew a packed house and proved he could still sing. His announcement of the final encore was rather touching— "Evening Star" from *Tannhauser,* "which I have sung many times on the stage, and used to enjoy doing."

The Tokyo baseball club was training at Casa Grande. United States major leaguers couldn't believe it when they saw the Japanese practicing for more than six hours, but they told the Americans that back in Japan they train from 9 A.M. to 5 P.M. This is the way their musicians practice, too! (I was impressed by the way the desert does much with little, instead of little with much.)

Mrs. Cook and I had a pleasant luncheon with the Tucson Music Teachers Association in Levy's Fiesta Room, where I spoke on Basic Principles of Suzuki Talent Education. We enjoyed hearing a Family Concert by the Phoenix Symphony under its conductor, Philip Spurgeon. Both Phil and his wife Julia were Oberlin grads whom I had known years ago. He did a good, musical job, with effective programming and commentary. It was good to see them again, and we enjoyed meeting the concertmaster, Richard Posner.

The Tucson Symphony under Gregory Millar gave a concert with Hans Richter-Haaser, the capable piano soloist. A critic wrote, "It is the finest community orchestra in the land." I wondered—who would be prepared to pass judgment on such a matter?

The Arizona Chamber Orchestra under Dean Robert Hull

gave a Connoisseur Concert in Crowder Hall. After three faculty soloists had played with the orchestra, it performed the Proko-fieff Classical Symphony. For an encore, a movement of the Pro-kofieff was repeated "to see how fast they can play it."

The Friends of Music presented the Tel Aviv String Quartet with a clarinetist, all members of the Israel Philharmonic. This was a good ensemble, with the Brahms *Clarinet Quintet* the high point of their concert. The Tucson High School All-City Orches-tra Festival showed a wide range in quality. The musical *1776* was different and enjoyable. Its ending, with the group posed as in the famous picture of the Continental Congress, is effective, but the music is far from memorable.

The All-State Concert at the University presented five organ-izations composed of selected high school students. It was much too long. The AAA choral conductor was excellent. Paul Sala-munovich made music all the time. The orchestra conductor was my friend, Marvin Rabin. He did Copland's *Quiet City* and movements three and four from the Dvorak *Symphony No. 4, as they should be done,* not the way I had heard in Albuquerque. It is always a pleasure to see and hear Marvin.

The University sponsored a three-day string symposium. Win-ners were Nicolas Grant, violin, of San Diego, California, and Harry Clark, cello, of Austin, Texas. They played with the Uni-versity Orchestra the Saint-Saëns *Violin Concerto* and Tchaikov-sky's *Rococo Variations.* The judges for the contest and clinicians for the symposium were Joachim Chassman and Michael Rabin, violin, and Raya Garbousova, cello.

Mr. Chassman advised a student: "*Play* Mozart, don't work him." And he reported that once when Heifetz implored his pianist, "Can't you play it faster?" Emmanuel Bay replied, "Yes, but the keys won't come back faster." Chassman invited me to dinner in Los Angeles, "where they have earthquakes." (I call them the "L.A. tremolo"—one of California's many faults.)

Michael Rabin, a fine violinist, was able to relate well with college students. He called Wieniawski the "Chopin of the violin," and kept after students to "Do something with it!" His soft voice and quiet teaching manner reminded me of his own teacher, Ivan Galamian. Certainly, as I visited with him, the thought never crossed my mind that this young man would be dead in less than a year.

Madame Garbousova could still play the cello. As she demonstrated a passage in very high harmonics, she described the feeling of "three thousand people waiting for a mistake." She advised a girl cellist never to come on stage in a miniskirt. (She had showed the women of the Sioux City Orchestra years ago how to play cello "continental," not side-saddle!) She told a student to trill lighter, "like a butterfly." How about a humming-bird?

All too soon, the time came for us to leave the desert, the saguaros, and the many-colored mountains. And so, armed with big hat, desert boots, and electric blanket, the "slowest gun in the West" (but still alive) rode off into the sunrise.

III. *Winter Wonderland* (1971-72)

Winter Haven, Florida, was our very pleasant home for the first three months of 1972. In the citrus belt of Central Florida, with a chain of lakes scattered throughout, this town provided a welcome change from the traffic jams of the cities and made a fine base for our jaunts to Disney World, Cypress Gardens, the Bok Tower, many cities, etc.

We spent three weeks getting there, via Washington, D.C.; Williamsburg, Va.; Greenville and Chapel Hill, N.C.; Spartanburg, Columbia, and Charleston, S.C., and other pleasant stops for visits, short workshops, etc. On the way home we visited more gardens in Charleston, workshopped at the University of North Carolina in Chapel Hill, stopped at Berea College in Kentucky, and completed our delightful four-month winter in a relaxed fashion. Many interesting details might be written about our experiences, but this book is becoming quite lengthy, so I'll be brief.

Thinking back, this might be called the "Winter of the Dvorak Cello Concerto." December 11 in the Concert Hall of the new Kennedy Center for the Performing Arts in Washington we heard

the National Symphony under Howard Mitchell play the Dvorak
with Christine Walevska, a young Californian, as soloist. (The
fact that conducted tours of the Center were stopped because
of thievery the day after we went through should not be mis-
interpreted. It was pure coincidence!)

February 17 in Dade County Auditorium, Miami, we heard
the London Symphony under André Previn, with sixteen-year-old
Lawrence Foster as soloist in the Dvorak.

March 16 in the Municipal Auditorium, Orlando, we heard
the Florida Symphony under Pavle Despalj, with Pierre Fournier
the excellent soloist in the Dvorak *Cello Concerto*.

As if this were not enough, one evening when we were watching Educational TV from Tampa, a foreign movie was shown
which used this Concerto as its "theme"!

On November 16 we had gone in to Severance Hall to visit
Michael Rabin and to hear him play Bruch's *Scottish Fantasy*
with the Cleveland Orchestra under Arthur Fiedler. January 20
we went to Orlando for the Florida Symphony concert. The
program that night pictured Rabin and announced that he would
play the *Scottish Fantasy* and the Glazounov *Violin Concerto*
at the next concert, February 10. An announcement from the
stage told of his death in New York the previous night, and said
Young Uck Kim would substitute for him. Dead at thirty-five—
what a pity! How much talent, hard work, experience, and
promise were snuffed out at such an early age!

Signs of the times: The St. Petersburg Civic Music Association folded, stopping its sponsorship of series of concerts. The
St. Petersburg Chamber Music Society disbanded, giving its
remaining funds to the Gulf Coast Symphony. Winter Haven
had no concert series this year, for the first time in a long while.
The greatest enthusiasm of players and supporters (Symphony
Guild, etc.), attendance and interest of *young people* were for
the worst orchestra we heard during the year. More food for
thought!

Chapter XXVII

How It Began—How It Should End—Finale

(From the Winter, 1966 issue of the *American String Teacher*, in a series on this subect):

How It Began . . .

I first heard violins play in a small high school orchestra performing at the opening of a new store in our village. As I stood watching the violinists I was especially entranced by their sound in a piece called "The Japanese Sandman." So I began to study violin with the conductor, who was also principal of the high school.

Perhaps there was some connection between this first orchestral selection and my later having Shinichi Suzuki at Oberlin twice, as well as four young Japanese violin teachers to work with Oberlin children.—*Clifford A. Cook*

How It Should End . . .

(From "Music For a Funeral" by Howard M. Van Sickle, in the *American String Teacher,* Winter, 1970):

The reply from Clifford A. Cook revealed his delightful touch of humor when part of his response was on the order of "There'll Be A Hot Time. . . ." In a more serious vein, however, he said he would pick the slow movement (Adagio) from the Brahms *Sonata in D minor.*

Finale . . .

Music is a "vanishing art"—as fast as it is produced, the sound evaporates and disappears. Musical performance is like a story, written on a blackboard and erased as fast as it is written.

The "embalming" tape catches some of the spirit of a performance, but not all—just as a corpse suggests a departed spirit, but does not contain it. Where music's effect *can* last, however, is in the innermost depths of man's spirit, *the very core of his being*. What a privilege it has been to serve such an art!

Acknowledgments

"Thoughts on Private Teaching" first appeared in the *American Music Teacher* for September-October, 1961. "Improving String Ensemble Repertoire" was originally printed in *The Instrumentalist* for February, 1960. "Cello Teaching by Violinists" appeared in the *American String Teacher*, January, 1960; "Composite Report from the American Suzuki Institute" was published in the Summer, 1972, issue of the same magazine. Other reprints were noted as they occurred in the text. Reviews, interviews, quotes, etc., were credited to authors and/or publications when possible. Thanks for the music notation and the back-cover photograph go to Professor Arthur Montzka.

My deep gratitude goes to the many generous people and sources contributing to this book. The patience, interest, typing and editing help of my wife have been beyond belief!

—Clifford A. Cook

Oberlin, Ohio
1972

APPENDIX A
Personnel in Festival String Orchestras
1955 (1), 1957 (2), 1958 (3), 1959 (4), 1961 (5), 1965 (6), 1966 (7)

VIOLIN

Adams, Julia 4, 5
Adams, Laura 2, 3(Va.)
Adams, Sue 2
Alvarez, Phillip 1
Apsey, Virginia 4
Arnold, Judith 3, 4, 5
Arnold, Peggy 1, 2, 3
Baker, Anne 3
Baker, Carol 6
Barker, Jean 2
Barlow, Joan 5
Barnaj (Hoça), William 1, 2, 3, 4, 5
Basinger, Emily 5
Bayer, Enid 2(Va.), 3
Beckett, John 1, 6, 7
Beckett, Wendy 7
Behnke, Elizabeth 7
Belchetz, Ruth 7
Bell, Jack 6
Bernhardt, Donald 1, 2
Berthelon, Georgia 5(Vc.), 6
Bias, Joan 1
Bickel, Raymond 7
Bishop, Marywynn 4
Blackwell, Scilla 6
Blank, Joan 2
Bolender, Susanne 7
Bonhoeffer, Cornelie 3
Borkowski, Francis 1
Borley, Barbara 6, 7

Bos, Marilyn 1, 2
Boyce, Gloria 1
Brenneman, Cheryl 5
Broggini, Ray 7
Brooks, Bruce 1, 2
Brouwer, Margaret 4
Brown, Phillipa 5
Brown, Rebecca 6
Brown, Robert 3
Buck, David 7
Buck, Mrs. Robina 1, 3, 4
Buckingham, Roberta 3
Bukovac, Barbara 1, 2, 3, 4
Burky, Kenneth 3, 4
Burnett, Kenneth 2, 3
Byers, Harold 6
Campbell, Christine 1
Carlson, Fred 1
Carol, Jean 1
Carroll, Mary Alice 3
Casada, Tom 4
Case, Evan 5
Cerone, Linda 6
Christian, Catherine 5
Clapp, Stephen 3, 4
Clark, Cathy 7
Clark, Linda 5
Cleary, Carl 4
Cleary, Nelson 4
Cleveland, Dennis 6
Clymer, Ann 3

220

VIOLIN *(Cont.)*

Connell, Elizabeth 4
Cook, Judith 3
Cook, Merrilyn 4
Courtley, Darrell 6
Craig, Jean 1, 2, 3
Cramer, Jenny 5, 6, 7
Cramer, Sally 2, 3, 5
Crayton, John 3
Crissey, Susan 6
Crosby, Ardella 1
Crosby, Constance 2
Culp, Paula 5
Currier, Susanne 7
Davis, Claire 2
Davis, Phillip 6
Davis, Sidney 6
De Falco, Frank 1 (Db.), 2
Dixon, Mrs. Elizabeth 1, 2, 3, 5
Dixon, Linda 1, 2, 3
Dixon, Robert 3
Dougherty, Melissa 1, 2, 3, 4
Douglas, Susan 1, 2
Douglass, Wayne 3, 4
Dove, James 4
Downs, Donald 4
Dudley, Mary Ann 4
Dugan, Mary Alice 5, 6 (Va.)
Dugas, Francine 6
Dunie, Eileen 1
Duran, Pat 7
Dyson, Martha 5
Eder, Sheila 6
Eisenberg, Vida 7
Elmer, Geraldine 4
Ergezi, Ernest 7
Everett, Peggy 7
Fabricant, Ruth 3
Falk, Nina 6, 7
Faulkner, Diana 2, 4
Fax, Jane 4
Fetzer, Nita 7
Field, Constance 1
Fielder, Amy 3, 4 (Db.), 5

Fiske, Richard 1
Fonda, Tom 1
Foote, Lillian 1, 2, 3, 4
Ford, Judy 5
Foreman, Murray 7
Fossenkemper, Mrs. Neva 6
Foster, Genette 6
Fountain, Robert 1, 2, 3, 4
Frame, Barbara 5
Franks, Marcia 5
Frech, Jo Ann 7
Fuchs, Louanne 3, 4
Fulkerson, Gregory 7
Gage, Carolyn 1
Galambos, Joan 5
Gamble, Leslie 6
Gates, Margaret 6, 7
Gerber, Timothy 7
Gilbert, Larry 7
Glasow, Ann 2, 3
Glazier, Laura 4
Gleason, Gilbert 1, 2
Gleason, Polly 5
Goddard, Debbie 7
Goerlich, Alfred 1, 2
Goichberg, Rena 7
Goldberg, Eugene 5
Goldenberg, Alice 1
Gottlieb, David 7
Gouse, Nancy 3, 4, 5
Gray, Nelson 1
Green, Edward 1 (Db.), 2
Greenbaum, Sheryl 6, 7
Grey, Charles 2, 3
Griffin, Elisabeth 1
Griffin, Patricia 1
Grigg, John 2 (Db.), 3, 4
Gushin, Margo 5, 6
Gutsche, Myra Lee 1
Hadden, Valerie 3
Hagen, Katherine 2
Hagstrom, Katherine 2, 3
Haight, Christine 2, 3

Violin *(Cont.)*

Hall, Emily 1
Hanak, Mary Ann 4, 5
Hanawalt, Nancy 1, 2, 3
Handyside, Hilary 3, 4, 5
Hanlin, Ruth 4
Hanmer, Linda 1, 2
Havranek, Roger 1
Haworth, Ann 5
Hayes, Barbara 5
Hayes, Deborah 4
Hayes, Jeanine 3, 4, 5
Hayes, Lauretta 6
Hecock, Christine 1
Herman, Paul 6
Hoff, Deborah 6
Hoffmann, Richard 1
Hogg, Beth 4, 5
Holbrook, Richard 1, 2, 3, 4
Holliman, Jamesetta 2, 3
Hoover, C. 4
Hopkins, J. 4
Houck, Annette 1, 2
Houck, Mary 3
Houser, Susan 3
Housh, Cynthia 7
Howard, Mrs. Larrie 1
Hudson, Mrs. Bonnie 6, 7
Huff, Marilyn 4
Hunkins, Nancy 3, 4, 5
Hunt, Anita 5
Hunter, Nancy 7
Hutchison, Jane 1
Huxoll, Sharon 2, 3
Ikenouchi, Mutsuko 6, 7
Isaacson, Mrs. Helen 1
Jackson, Gordon 2
Jakey, Lauren 1, 2, 3, 4
Jensen, Beverly 4
Johnson, Emily 6, 7
Johnson, Fred 1, 2, 3
Johnson, Mrs. Hugh 7
Johnson, Margaret 1, 2, 3, 4
Johnson, Sherry 1, 2, 3, 4

Johnson, Susan 6
Jones, Harold 5
Jones, Helen 4
Jones, Prudence 3
Joseph, Bette 2, 3
Josephs, Christine 7
Joy, N. 4
Judson, Barbara 1, 2, 3, 4
Kahn, Nathaniel 2
Kay, Bonnie 5
Kazmierzak, David 4
Kelley, Dolly 4, 5
Kendall, Mary Ann 1
Kidder, Caroyln 5
King, Rebecca 2, 3
(Mrs. Rebecca Chudacoff) 6 (Va.)
Kingman, Louis 6
Kinsey, Carlyn 4
Kirtley, Carol 5
Klarr, Norma 3, 4
Knolle, Ekard 3
Koenig, Theodore 2
Kolden, Martha 6
Kort, Carol 3
Kramer, Larry 3
Krauss, Raymond 5
Krepps, Lyn 1
Krinitz, Dorothy 4
Krivell, Harold 5
Kunze, Judy 4
Langworthy, Elise 2, 3
Lemcke, Sharon 6
Lenno, Bruce 2 (Db.), 3(Va.), 4
Liersch, Nancy 5
Liu, Nien-Lung 1, 2, 3
Lloyd, Anne 2
Locke, Joanne 3
Long, Joan 1
Ludewig, Elsa 1
Lyman, Janet 1, 2, 3
McAlonan, Jane 5
McClung, Thomas 7
McDonald, Grace 1, 2, 3

VIOLIN *(Cont.)*

McGaugh, Bonnie 5
McKenzie, Jane 2
McLarnan, Nancy 3
McRoberts, Peggy 5
Macarthy, Mary 2
Mack, Dorothy 1
Maraffie, Frederick 5, 6
Marschner, Erica 6
Marsh, David 6
Martin, Cidney 3
Mary Louis, Sister 6
Mathers, Anne 5
Matlow, Austin 1, 2
Matsuki, Miyako 2, 3, 4
Mauney, Cindy 6
Mauney, Dorothy 6, 7
Mauney, Phyllis 6, 7
Mayall, Mary Ann 5
Mazurek, Frank 1, 2, 3
Meek, Charles 5
Meek, David 5
Meek, Dorothy 5
Meek, Lowell 5
Megyesi, Maxine 3, 4(Vc.), 5
Mendy, Allen 7
Meseroll, Robert 1
Meyer, Coleen 1, 2
Miller, Richard 1, 2, 3, 4, 5, 6, 7
Mochizuki, Kenji 1
Molison, Robert 2
Montzka, Arthur 1, 2
Moore, Ellen 6, 7
Moore, Jane 1
Moore, Kathy 1, 2, 3, 4, 6
Moore, Ronald 5
Moran, Carol 7
Morgan, Katherine 4
Murphy, Mary Pat 4, 5
Nadig, Barbara 1
Natterer, Gail 1
Nelson, Karla 2, 3
Nesbitt, Holly 2, 3
Nichols, Carolyn 6

Nichols, Maxine 6
Niehl, Betsy 1, 2
Noel, Ella 5
Numanami, Kazuko 7
Olson, Doris 2, 3, 5
Olson, Eric 6
Orr, Phyllis 5
Orttung, Evie 2(Vc.), 3
Ostrander, Linda 3
Parks, Susan 3, 4, 5
Payne, Ruth 1, 2
Pearlman, Carol 3
Pease, Nancy 5
Pendergraft, Sara 2
Peters, Irene 6
Pettiford, Cheryl 2
Pfohl, Alice 1, 2
Pierce, Catherine 2, 3(Va.), 4
Pollack, Rosallyn 6
Pontious, Melvin 2
Powell, Ellen 6
Pratt, Anne 2
Presler, Marianna 1
Rabinovitz, Ruth 5
Ramman, Philip 5
Rautenberg, John 1(Vc.), 2
Raynor, Elizabeth 2, 3
Read, Thomas 2, 3
Reitz, Howard 2, 3
Renne, Joan 2, 4 & 5(Va.)
Restemyer, Carol 2
Riccardi, Richard 5
Richard, Julie 1, 2
Robertson, David 1, 2
Robertson, Gail 1, 2, 3, 4, 6
Roby, Paul 1, 2, 3
Rodgers, Delta 5
Rogers, Helen 6
Roose, Kirk 3
Rose, Patricia 2
Rouslin, Daniel 6
Roxin, Charles 6, 7
Rubis, George 3, 4 & 5(Va.)

Violin *(Cont.)*

Rutman, Davida 6
Rylands, Ann 4, 5
Sacco, Peter 7
Sanders, Betsy 6
Scheiber, Peter 2
Schenkman, Lucy 5
Schettler, Hebe 1, 3(Db.)
Schmidt, Rodney 3, 4, 5
Schwarz, Sandra 6, 7
Schwinn, Marilynn 5
Scott, Helen 1
Scott, John 5
Sepsenwol, Noah 5
Shakes, Joseph 1
Shipps, Joan 2(Va.), 3
Shive, Carol 7
Shrider, Larry 2
Sigl, Lenore 1, 2
Skinner, Joan 3, 4
Smith, Julian 7
Smith, Patty 1, 2, 3, 4
Smith, Wesley 1, 2, 3, 5
Snook, Carolyn 4
Snyder, Edgar 5
Spotts, Roberta 3, 4
Spotts, Lynn 5
Sprunger, Donna 6, 7
Sprunger, Ron 5
Spurlock, Ann 2
Stephens, Emily 2
Sterling, Marianne 6
Stoakes, Carolyn 4
Stoddart, Joseph 6
Stoffer, Anne 2
Stokes, Mary Beth 3, 4
Stoll, Nancy 1, 2, 3, 7
Strahl, Marilyn 1
Stulberg, Bernard 7
Stunkel, Marcia 2(Va.), 3
Super, Darlene 1, 2, 3
Suzuki, Eiko 7
Swartz, Donna Dee 6
Sweigart, Esther 1

Szatrowski, Ted 7
Tanner, Deon 6
Tanner, Joanne 6
Thompson, Tamara 1
Threatte, Leslie 5
Tischke, Martha 1
Tkach, D. 4
Toba, Hiroko 6
Tominari, Kumiko 6, 7
Tongg, Geraldine 1, 2
Townsend, Barbara 3
Treiber, Carolyn 2
Tripp, Susan 5
Tryon, Karen 6
Turco, Mrs. Wilma 1, 2
VanEngen, Keitha 2
Wachtler, Laura 6
Waldman, Harvey 1, 2, 3, 4
Walker, Maralee 1
Warch, Pauline 3, 4, 5
Wasserman, Sandra 1, 2, 3, 4, 5
Weinstock, Frank 6, 7
Weisman, Marcia 2(Va.), 3
Welch, Betty 6, 7
Wenzel, Henry 5, 6
West, George 3
Wharry, Roslyn 2
Wheeler, Candy 6, 7
Whicker, Gene 5
Whiteside, Cassie 4, 5, 6
Whiteside, Louise 6, 7
Wilhoyt, Brittania 4
Wilkerson, Rose 2
Williams, Arthur 1, 2, 3, 4, 5, 6
Williams, Elizabeth 4, 5
Williams, Janet 4
Wilson, Joyce 5
Winters, James 3
Wolf, Eleanor 5
Wood, Lynn 1, 4(Va.)
Workman, Dianne 3
Yamada, Hiroko 6
Yamashiro, Naomi 1

VIOLIN *(Cont.)*

Yinger, Nancy 6, 7

Younkin, Norma 7

Zander, Patricia 7

Zimmerman, Carla 1, 2, 3, 4, 5

Zinman, David 1 (Va.), 2, 3

VIOLA

Ackert, Roger 6

Allshouse, Charlet 7

Andrews, Robert 7

Arnold, Joyce 1

Ballinger, James S. 4, 5

Ballou, Edmond 7

Bassett, Richard 6

Bates, Mary 2

Baty, Carol 4

Behrman, Sydney 4

Bennett, Lunetta 7

Berman, Mrs. Estelle 3, 4, 5

Bernhardt, Barbara 1

Berry, Margaret 6, 7

Bjerre, Sandra 2

Boggs, Clara 4

Bovee, Barbara 4

Brice, Martha 1

Bromund, Mary Lee 3, 4, 5

Buie, Julia 5

Butler, Melvin 6, 7

Charley, Alfred 3

Chitambar, Charlene 3

Christman, Karen 5

Cole, Bonnie 4

Compton, Catherine 7

D'Agostino, Philip 7

Dolan, Cornelia 5

Dolan, Diane 5

Edwards, Darrell 7

Ehrlich, Don 5

Evans, Robert 6

Feldman, Lynne 6(Vc.), 7

Foley, Richard 5

Follett, Robert 5

Fordyce, James 7

Foster, William 6

Fousek, Blanche 1

Friedman, Elaine 5

Gerson, Katherine 3, 4, 5

Gettig, Carl 4

Gibbs, Leonard 4

Graves, Marilyn 1

Grobel, Stella 5

Gustafson, Roger 4

Hake, Katherine 4

Hall, Catherine 6

Hall, Margaret 6

Harbison, William 7

Harris, Gwendolyn 2

Heard, Charles 1

Henderson, Jane 7

Herriott, Alison 1

Hine, Roberta 2, 3

Hirsch, Sue 1

Hoffman, Mary Ann 5

Holbrook, Deborah 1, 2, 3, 4, 5

Holbrook, Mrs. Dorothy 1,2, 4, 5

Huggins, Faye 7

Jones, Tyrone 7

Kalb, Debbie 7

Kanner, Mary 7

Kessler, Sandra 3

King, Sylvia 2, 3

Krasner, Vivien 5

Kremer, Mary 2

Kvistad, Richard 6

Laffredo, Warren 2

Laster, Marva 1

Lawall, Martha 1

Lejonhud, Carolyn 1

Leonard, Kathryn 1, 2

Lo, Adrian 7

Lowry, Lynette 5

VIOLA *(Cont.)*

Lubin, Alan 1, 3
McCandless, Nancy 1, 2, 3, 4
McKenney, Carol 6
Makman, Richard 1
Marden, Eunice 2
Martin, Meredith 4
Mattson, Sara 2, 3, 5
Maze, Robert 5
Meek, Richard 5
Millard, Sally 2, 3
Miller, David 7
Moore, Charlene 2, 3
Morlan, Richard 5
Mostovoy, Stephanie 6, 7
Ogden, Jean 1, 2
Orenstein, Martha 1
Orr, Colleen 7
Owens, Marilyn 2, 3
Page, Coin 7
Pasquale, Benjamin 1, 2
Pearson, Juanita 1
Pineo, Sharon 6
Price, Stephen 7
Reuper, Doris 5
Rhinehart, Richard 3
Robb, Nancy 3

Russell, Douglas 3
Schnerer, Gary 1, 2, 3
Severs, Karen 7
Shackford, Martha 7
Shaner, Thomas 1
Spoor, Mary Ann 3
Stechow, Wolfgang 1
Steg, Mrs. Barbara 1, 2, 3
Steg, Paul 1, 2, 3
Stoffel, Ruth 5
Tamblyn, Paul 2 (Db.), 3
Taylor, Peggy 4, 5
Thompson, Patricia 3
Traylor, Benjamin 6
Wade, Ruth 7
Waldman, Glenys 6, 7
White, Mary 2
Wiens, Diane 3, 4, 5
Wilder, Mary Flo 3
Williams, Ralph 6
Woods, Katherine 4
Woodward, Ann 4
Yeomans, David 3
Yonley, Fred, Jr. 6, 7
Zenge, Michael 5

VIOLONCELLO

Andrews, Ruth 6
Arnold, Caroline 1, 2, 3
Banks, Elaine 7
Bardo, Lucy 2, 3, 5
Barron, Carol 7
Beal, Stephanie 7
Bergfald, Anne 2, 3
Bierbaum, Caryl 3
Bradley, Barbara 4
Brazinski, Frank 2
Brecher, John 3
Brooke, Margaret 4
Brown, Peter 1, 2
Bruderer, Conrad 3

Buck, Richard 1, 2, 3, 4
Busser, Carol 5
Butters, Diane 3
Byers, Louise 7
Chan, Marjorie 3, 4, 5
Christenson, Barbro 3
Church, Frank 1, 2, 3, 4
Clark, R. 4
Clough, Linda 7
Colman, Marylee 1
Conway, Sally 4
Cook, Stella 4
Danforth, Douglas 5
Davidson, Carol 1

VIOLONCELLO *(Cont.)*

Deahl, Robert 2
Deardorff, Joanne 2
Drucker, Kathleen 1, 2
Dyson, Barbara 5
Edelmann, Alice 1
Emanuels, Roger 5
Fanos, Stavroula 1
Faris, Eleanor 5
Farrar, Rodney 6
Finckel, Michael 6
Flatgaard, Marie 6
Folden, Wanda 2
Follows, Arthur 1
Gardner, Linda 2
Gilbert, Joan 2, 3
Giltner, Kathleen 5
Graham, Philip 4
Griffith, Charles 2, 3
Guenther, Marinell 1
Guthrie, Ward 7
Hall, Harvey 2
Harrington, Barbara 4
Haskell, Tamme 7
Hester, Richard 7
Hiu, Mariette 1
Hocks, Christian 7
Holbrook, Clyde 1, 2, 4
Howard, Peter 1
Huffman, Martha 7
Hunkins, Arthur 2
Isele, David 7
Ives, Ronalee 6
Johnston, Taylor 6
Jones, Gwen 5
Kendall, Nancy 6
Kennedy, Emily 4
Kline, Susan 7
Konney, William 6
Laise, Jean 1, 3
Landreville, Lynn 2
Larson, Catherine 6
Lewis, Ellen 7
Long, Krista 7

McClinton, Joe 7
McElvain, Judith 3
McIntosh, Bruce 6, 7
McLaughlin, Elizabeth 7
Mack, George 2, 3, 4
Maslanka, David 6
Matchett, Jane 2, 3, 4
Matsoukas, Euthemia 5
Meek, Barbara 5
Meisel, Nancy 3, 4, 5
Meisels, Florence 5
Metcalf, Gail 6
Meyers, James 7
Middleton, Polly 6
Moore, Mrs. Jean 1, 2, 3, 4, 5, 6
Moore, Melissa 1
Mumma, Karen 3, 4, 5
Murphy, Charles 1, 3
Murray, Laurie 3, 4
Myers, Patricia 5
Nevins, Elizabeth 4
Norton, Jean 5
Ogg, Sandra 6, 7
Otts, Sally 7
Owen, John 3, 4
Owens, Dianne 7
Padelford, Carolyn 1
Pearson, Elizabeth 6, 7
Pettijohn, Clare 4
Pintur, Sandra 1, 2, 4
Plum, Deloris 4
Powell, Constance 6
Powell, Patricia 2
Reeve, Douglas 4, 5
Reeves, Nancy 2
Reilender, Ernestine 1
Reitz, Judy 4
Rhea, Christine 5
Rice, Gwendolyn 5
Robertson, Jean 1, 2
Roose, Debbie 5
Rylands, Mary Lou 5
Sabo, Marlee Jo 5

Violoncello *(Cont.)*

Sargent, Anita 2
Schettler, Ted 1
Schlecht, Clara 1
Schnelker, Cathy 6
Schwimmer, Betty 3
Seaman, George 6
Sentieri, Richard 6
Sherin, Harry 4
Sholz, Edwin 1, 2
Shufro, Joseph 6, 7
Silverman, Fred 6
Simcox, Mark 7
Slater, Ann 2, 3
Slezak, Eugenia 4, 5
Smith, Shirley 1
Socolofsky, David 6
Spurgeon, Phillip 3
Stallone, Thomas 7
Stechow, Nicola 1, 2
Stewart, Carol 2

Stock, Lynne 3
Sturgis, Ruth 7
Tanger, Shirley 7
Thompson, Cynthia 4
Toth, Andor, Jr. 7
Truitt, Rebecca 1, 2, 3
Turner, Prue 6
Vail, Phyllis 1
Waln, Ronald 1
Walton, Brian 4, 5
Warch, Willard 2, 3, 4, 5, 6
Weinstock, Robert 7
Wien, Norman 3
Williamson, Joanne 7
Wishart, Sondra 1
Wolcott, Mary 7
Wood, Mrs. Carol 1
Wright, Carol 1
Yee, Barbara 5

Double Bass

Allen, Roy 6
Berman, Eric 7
Bozicenic, Roland 7
Braun, Linda 4
Bravine, Curtiss 6, 7
Brown, Robert 2
Brubaker, David 4
Bryant, Charles 1
Butt, Edgar 3
Chase, Marian 7
Cherry, James 1
Clark, Linda 7
Coates, Christopher 3
Cooper, Kathryn 1
Cramer, Paul 6
Danesi, David 3, 4, 5
Davis, Barbara 4
Davis, Jerry 5
Davis, Nancy 7
Davis, Sharon 6

Dexter, Carolyn 1
Duncan, James 3
Easter, Wallace 7
Erlenbach, Julius 6
Eubank, Lee 1, 2, 3, 4
Feldmeyer, Don 1
Ferguson, Elizabeth 4
Ferris, Lawrence 6
Fox, Russell 7
Fratena, Roger 7
Gardner, James 5
Gogolak, Edward 7
Goldthwaite, Thomas 2
Groff, James 6
Handyside, Douglas 3, 4, 5, 7
Harding, John 4
Hargrave, Susan 6
Harrity, Lee 1, 2
Hedling, Fred 3
Hoça, George 4, 5

DOUBLE BASS *(Cont.)*

Hutsko, Paul 5
Jackson, Robert 6
Jacobson, Glenn 1, 2
Jahn, Theodore 5
Johnson, Patricia 3
Judkins, Janet 1
Keip, Katherine 5
Knowles, Carolyn 1, 2, 3
Kroll, Jack 1
Laber, Robert 6
Latosek, Linda 7
Laubly, Anamarie 5
Lee, Jim 5
Lengnick, Henry 2, 3
Loud, Barbara 3
Mandel, Paula 5
Mayo, Kitty 7
Morse, William 6

Muller, Lynda 5
Murphy, Richard 2, 5
Naser, Gisela 3
O'Donnell, Thomas 3
Ortner, John 6
Porter, William 1
Poulton, James 5
Roellinger, Margaret 2, 3, 4
Rogers, Reginald 7
Ross, Kenneth 3, 4
Schoeninger, Kenneth 5
Storch, Howard 3, 4
Strong, Francis 6
Thies, Thomas 6
Thurman, Geraldine 1
VanLeuvan, Alice 1
Wilson, Ollie 7

PIANO

Moyer, David 3

Lloyd, Norman 6

ELECTRIC TUNER

Naumann, Linda 5

APPENDIX B
Short Selected Bibliography on the
Talent Education of Shinichi Suzuki

Talent Education and Suzuki by John D. Kendall, Music Educators National Conference, Washington, D. C., 1966, pp. 24.

The Suzuki Method Adapted for Class Teaching in the Bedford Public Schools by Diana Tillson, Mt. Kisco, N. Y., 1967, pp. 35.

Talent Education News, Vols. I-III, edited by (Carl Shultz and) Howard M. Van Sickle, Mankato, Minn., 1968-1971.

Nurtured by Love by Shinichi Suzuki (translation by Waltraud Suzuki), Exposition Press, Jericho, N.Y., 1969, pp. 121.

Project Super, 1966-68 by Virginia Frye Wensel, Eastman School of Music, Rochester, N. Y., Revised Edition, 1970, pp. 85.

Suzuki Education in Action by Clifford A. Cook, Exposition Press, Jericho, N. Y., 1970, pp. 114.

Talent Education (A Program for Early Development) by Masaaki Honda, Early Development Association, Tokyo, Japan, 1970, pp. 53.

Suzuki Series (3 articles) by Margery V. Aber in "Wheel of Delta Omicron," Menasha, Wisc., 1971.

The Suzuki Approach (a continuing series, published monthly) by Louise Behrend in "Allegro," Associated Musicians of Greater New York, N. Y., beginning November, 1971.

Suzuki in the String Class by Paul Zahtilla (Teacher's Manual, Violin, Viola, Cello, Bass books, Records), Summy-Birchard Co., Evanston, Ill., 1972.

Note: Magazine and newspaper articles by the hundreds on phases of this subject have appeared since 1958. It is impractical to list them here.

APPENDIX C
Some Selected Orchestra Suggestions

FLEXIBLE SCORING FOR YOUNG ORCHESTRA

Bartók   *Five Pieces for Younger Orchestras*   Remick
          Six Pieces for Younger Orchestras
Riegger   *Suite for Younger Orchestras*   Associated M. P.
Harris   *American Youth Orchestral Series*   Bourne
McKay   *Scenes from the Southwest*   Remick

Small Orchestra

Purcell-Bush   *The Fairy Queen* (Suite)   Mills Music
J. C. Bach   *Sinfonia in B-flat*   Peters
C. P. E. Bach-Steinberg   *Concerto in D*   Broude Bros.
Handel   *Organ Concerto No. 5*   Breitkopf & Härtel (AMP)
Rameau-Mottl   *Ballet Suite*   Broude Bros.
Boyce-Lambert   *Symphony No. 5*   Oxford University Press
Stamitz-Kindler   *Symphony in E-flat*   Elkan-Vogel
Haydn   *Sinfonia No. 36* (Diletto Musicale)   Doblinger
Haydn   *"London" Symphony in D*   AMP
        "Clock" Symphony
Mozart-Beecham   *Symphony No. 29 in A*   Boosey-Hawkes
Mozart   *Symphony Concertante* (Violin & Viola)   Breitkopf & Härtel (AMP)
Mozart   *Piano Concerto No. 24 in C minor*   Broude Bros.
Grétry-Mottl   *Ballet Suite*   Broude Bros.
Beethoven   *First Symphony in C*   Breitkopf & Härtel (AMP)
Schubert   *Symphony No. 5 in B-flat*   Breitkopf & Härtel (AMP)
Rossini   *Il Signor Bruschino Overture*   Carisch S. A.
Bartók   *Rumanian Folk Dances*   Boosey-Hawkes
Khachaturian-Bourdon   *Waltz from "Masquerade Suite"*   Leeds

Full Orchestra

Watters   *Our Own Orchestra Folio*   C. Fischer
   Our Junior Symphony Orchestra Folio
Watters   *Presser Youth Orchestra Folio*   Presser
Gordon   *Concert for Orchestra*   Bourne
   (Music through the Ages)
Jurey   *First Orchestra Program Album*   Mills Music
   Second Orchestra Program Album
Rebmann and Clark   *Master Series for Young Orchestras*   G. Schirmer
   (Suites from various composers' works)
Stock, Dasch, McConathy   *Symphony Series*   Silver, Burdett
   (arranged in concert programs)
Van Hoesen   *Living Music from the Past*   C. Fischer
Corelli-Müller   *Adagio and Allegro*   Ludwig
Kindler   *Three Seventeenth Century Dutch Tunes*   C. Fischer
Frescobaldi-Kindler   *Toccata*   Mills Music
Sammartini   *Symphony in D major*   Ludwig
Lully-Murphy   *French Baroque Suite*   Witmark
Couperin-Milhaud   *Overture and Allegro*   Elkan-Vogel
Whitney (arr.)   *Two Bach Airs*   Bourne
Bach-Cailliet   *Sheep May Safely Graze*   Boosey-Hawkes
Handel   *Grand Concerto in B-flat*   Music Press (Mercury)
Handel-Jacob   *Overture, Theodora*   J. Williams (Galaxy)
Whitney   *Variations on a Theme by Handel*   Witmark
Mozart   *Shepherd King Overture*   Boosey-Hawkes
Beethoven   *Egmont Overture*   Breitkopf & Härtel (AMP)
Dittersdorf-Kahn   *Tournament of Temperaments*   G. Schirmer
Piccini   *Didon Overture*   AMP
Piccini   *Overture to "The Good Daughter"*   Ludwig
Cimarosa-Schenkman   *Overture to "The Secret Marriage"*   G. Schirmer
Grétry   *Overture to "Céphale et Procris"*   Silver, Burdett
Grétry   *Overture to "Lucile"*   Ludwig
Gluck-Wagner   *Overture to "Iphigenia in Aulis"*   Breitkopf & Härtel (AMP)

Mendelssohn   *Symphony No. 1 in C minor*   Kalmus
Verdi   *La Forza Del Destino Overture*   Kalmus
Wagner   *Three Excerpts from "Die Meistersinger"*   Breitkopf
    & Härtel (AMP)
Johann Strauss-Lesinsky   *The Gipsy Baron Overture*   C. Fischer
Bizet   *Overture to "The Pearl Fishers"*   Sam Fox
Tchaikovsky   *Capriccio Italien*   Kalmus
Glière-Isaac   *Russian Sailors' Dance*   C. Fischer (original: Kalmus)
Saint-Saëns   *Introduction et Rondo Capriccioso,* violin and
    orchestra   Elkan-Vogel
Sibelius-Sopkin   *Finlandia*   C. Fischer
Van Hoesen   *Music of our Time*   C. Fischer
McKay   *Symphonie Miniature*   Summy-Birchard
McKay   *The Big Sky*   Boston Music Co.
Isaac   *South American Overture*   C. Fischer
Bergsma   *Paul Bunyan Suite*   C. Fischer
Grundman   *Two Sketches for Orchestra*   Boosey-Hawkes
Verall   *Symphony for Young Orchestras*   Boston Music Co.
Coates   *Knightsbridge March*   Chappell
Copland   *John Henry*   Boosey-Hawkes
Stravinsky   *Four Norwegian Moods*   AMP
Jacob   *Fantasia on the "Alleluia Hymn"*   J. Williams (Mills)
Britten   *Soirées Musicales*   Boosey-Hawkes
Hanson   *Love Duet from "Merry Mount"*   Harms
Anderson   *Bugler's Holiday*   Mills Music
    Sandpaper Ballet
    Serenata
Steg   *Symphony on Folk Songs*   Summy-Birchard
Rimer   *Fiddle Fun*   Charles Colin
Cowell   *Hymn and Fuguing Tune No. 3*   AMP
Loewe   *My Fair Lady (Highlights)*   Chappell
Rodgers-Bennett   *Flower Drum Song (Selection)*   William-
    son Music
Loewe-Bennett   *Camelot Selection*   Chappell
Bernstein-Müller   *West Side Story (Highlights)*   G. Schirmer
Holesovsky   *Bratislava*   Elkan-Vogel
    Prologue, Hymn and Dance   Elkan-Vogel

Gould   *American Salute*   Mills Music
Giannini   *Symphony No. 2*   Chappell
Diemer   *Youth Overture*   Mills Music
Washburn   *St. Lawrence Overture*   Boosey-Hawkes
Johnston   *Bunker Hill Fantasy*   Elkan-Vogel
Muczynski   *Dovetail Overture*   G. Schirmer

APPENDIX D
Additional Selected Bibliographies

(Not included in Chapter XVIII of my book, *String Teaching and Some Related Topics*)

A number of books, magazines, and newspapers have already been cited at appropriate points in this book. Here are a few additional useful sources on the strings and related subjects:

VIOLIN

Violins and Violinists by Franz Farga, Rockliff, London, 1950
Principles of Violin Playing and Teaching by Ivan Galamian, Prentice-Hall, 1962
The Twelve Lesson Course by Kato Havas, Bosworth, 1964
The Violin and I by Kato Havas, Bosworth, 1968
A Violinist's Notebook by Joseph Szigeti, Duckworth & Co., London, 1964
Szigeti on the Violin by Joseph Szigeti, Praeger, 1970
The History of Violin Playing (origins to 1761) by David Boyden, Oxford University Press, 1965
Memoirs by Carl Flesch, Rockliff, London, 1957
Violin Fingering—Its Theory and Practice by Carl Flesch, Dover, 1966
The Principles of Violin Fingering by I. M. Yampolsky, Oxford, 1967

(Cited now are a few records: Yehudi Menuhin, *Autobiography*; Ruggiero Ricci, *The Glory of Cremona*; Steven Staryk, *Traditional Études, Compositions by Wieniawski*)

Viola

The Art and Practice of Scale Playing on the Viola by William
Primrose, Mills Music, 1954
Basic Viola Technique by Melvin Berger, Leeds, 1966
The Viola: Guide for Teachers and Students by Henry Barrett,
University of Alabama, 1972
(Lillian Fuchs, *Bach Suites*, recorded complete.)

Violoncello

Cellist in Exile by Bernard Taper, McGraw-Hill, 1962
The Art of Cello Playing by Louis Potter, Jr., Summy-Birchard,
1964 (new edition due in 1973)
Cellist by Gregor Piatigorsky, Doubleday & Co., 1965
Joys and Sorrows by Pablo Casals and Albert Kahn, 1970
Head, Hand and Heart by Ida Roettinger, ASTA-Presser, 1970
(Pablo Casals, *Autobiography* record)

Double Bass

Comprehensive Catalogue of Literature for the String Bass by
Murray Grodner, Author, 1958
Introduction to the Double Bass by Raymond Elgar, Author,
1960
The String (Double) Bass by David Stanton, The Instrumentalist,
1965
The Fundamentals of Double Bass Playing by Barry Green,
Piper Co., 1972
(Bass recordings by Gary Karr, Bertram Turetzky, Barry Green
and others)

General

Violin Teaching in Class by Gertrude Collins, Oxford, 1962
Playing and Teaching Stringed Instruments (Parts 1 & 2) by
Matesky and Rush, Prentice-Hall, 1963-64
Planning the School String Program by Louis Trzcinski, Mills,
1963

String Problems, Players and Paucity (Tanglewood Symposia) edited by Louis Krasner, Syracuse University Press, 1965

Teaching Stringed Instruments in Classes by Elizabeth Green, Prentice-Hall, 1966

Carabo-Cone Concepts for Strings by Madeleine Carabo-Cone, Author, 1966-67

Menuhin's House of Music by Eric Fenby, Praeger, 1971

The Way They Play by Samuel and Sada Applebaum, Paganiniana, 1972

CONDUCTING

The Maestro (Toscanini) by Howard Taubman, Simon & Schuster, 1951

I Am A Conductor by Charles Munch, Oxford, 1955

Of Music and Music-Making by Bruno Walter, W. W. Norton, 1957

The Modern Conductor by Elizabeth Green, Prentice-Hall, 1961 and later

It's All In The Music by Doris Monteux, Farrar-Straus-Giroux, 1965

The Conductor's Art edited by Carl Bamberger, McGraw-Hill, 1965

The Cleveland Orchestra by Robert Marsh, World Publishing Co., 1967

The Great Conductors by Harold Schonberg, Simon & Schuster, 1967

Profiles (Cleveland Symphony Orchestra) by Joseph Wechsberg, *The New Yorker,* May 30, 1970

(Records: Bruno Walter *Rehearsals*
                   Pablo Casals *Rehearsals*
                   George Szell *Autobiography)*